DATE DUE

Terrorism 1

Terrorism

Hal Marcovitz

CHELSEA HOUSE PUBLISHERS
Philadelphia

Cover photos: front: Reuters/Corbis Bettman,
back: AP/Wide World Photos

Frontispiece: A police officer assists a woman
suffering from smoke inhalation after the World
Trade Center bombing, February 26, 1993.

CHELSEA HOUSE PUBLISHERS

Editor in Chief Stephen Reginald
Production Manager Pamela Loos
Art Director Sara Davis
Director of Photography Judy L. Hasday
Managing Editor James D. Gallagher
Senior Production Editor J. Christopher Higgins

Staff for TERRORISM

Senior Editor John Ziff
Associate Art Director Takeshi Takahashi
Designer Keith Trego
Picture Researcher Patricia Burns
Cover Designer Keith Trego

3 5 7 9 8 6 4

The Chelsea House World Wide Web address is
http://www.chelseahouse.com

Library of Congress Cataloging-in-Publication Data applied for

ISBN 0-7910-6914-1

Contents

GREAT DISASTERS
REFORMS and RAMIFICATIONS

Jill McCaffrey
National Chairman
Armed Forces Emergency Services
American Red Cross

Introduction

Disasters have always been a source of fascination and awe. Tales of a great flood that nearly wipes out all life are among humanity's oldest recorded stories, dating at least from the second millennium B.C., and they appear in cultures from the Middle East to the Arctic Circle to the southernmost tip of South America and the islands of Polynesia. Typically gods are at the center of these ancient disaster tales—which is perhaps not too surprising, given the fact that the tales originated during a time when human beings were at the mercy of natural forces they did not understand.

To a great extent, we still are at the mercy of nature, as anyone who reads the newspapers or watches nightly news broadcasts can attest.

Hurricanes, earthquakes, tornados, wildfires, and floods continue to exact a heavy toll in suffering and death, despite our considerable knowledge of the workings of the physical world. If science has offered only limited protection from the consequences of natural disasters, it has in no way diminished our fascination with them. Perhaps that's because the scale and power of natural disasters force us as individuals to confront our relatively insignificant place in the physical world and remind us of the fragility and transience of our lives. Perhaps it's because we can imagine ourselves in the midst of dire circumstances and wonder how we would respond. Perhaps it's because disasters seem to bring out the best and worst instincts of humanity: altruism and selfishness, courage and cowardice, generosity and greed.

As one of the national chairmen of the American Red Cross, a humanitarian organization that provides relief for victims of disasters, I have had the privilege of seeing some of humanity's best instincts. I have witnessed communities pulling together in the face of trauma; I have seen thousands of people answer the call to help total strangers in their time of need.

Of course, helping victims after a tragedy is not the only way, or even the best way, to deal with disaster. In many cases planning and preparation can minimize damage and loss of life—or even avoid a disaster entirely. For, as history repeatedly shows, many disasters are caused not by nature but by human folly, shortsightedness, and unethical conduct. For example, when a land developer wanted to create a lake for his exclusive resort club in Pennsylvania's Allegheny Mountains in 1880, he ignored expert warnings and cut corners in reconstructing an earthen dam. On May 31, 1889, the dam gave way, unleashing 20 million tons of water on the towns below. The Johnstown Flood, the deadliest in American history, claimed more than 2,200 lives. Greed and negligence would figure prominently in the Triangle Shirtwaist Company fire in 1911. Deplorable conditions in the garment sweatshop, along with a failure to give any thought to the safety of workers, led to the tragic deaths of 146 persons. Technology outstripped wisdom only a year later, when the designers of the luxury liner *Titanic* smugly declared their state-of-the-art ship "unsinkable," seeing no need to provide lifeboat capacity for everyone onboard. On the night of April 14, 1912, more than 1,500 passengers and crew paid for this hubris with their lives after the ship collided with an iceberg and sank. But human catastrophes aren't always the unforeseen consequences of carelessness or folly. In the 1940s the leaders of Nazi Germany purposefully and systematically set out to exterminate all Jews, along with Gypsies, homosexuals, the mentally ill, and other so-called undesirables. More recently terrorists have targeted random members of society, blowing up airplanes and buildings in an effort to advance their political agendas.

The books in the GREAT DISASTERS: REFORMS AND RAMIFICATIONS series examine these and other famous disasters, natural and human made. They explain the causes of the disasters, describe in detail how events unfolded, and paint vivid portraits of the people caught up in dangerous circumstances. But these books are more than just accounts of what happened to whom and why. For they place the disasters in historical perspective, showing how people's attitudes and actions changed and detailing the steps society took in the wake of each calamity. And in the end, the most important lesson we can learn from any disaster—as well as the most fitting tribute to those who suffered and died—is how to avoid a repeat in the future.

The Man
in the
White Hat

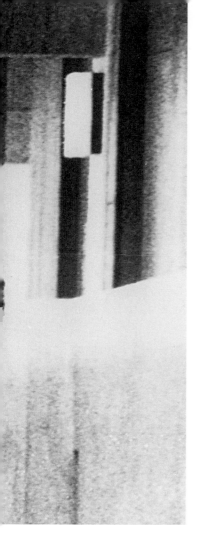

The leader of a squad of Palestinian terrorists holding nine Israeli Olympic athletes hostage gestures to a negotiator, Munich, West Germany, September 5, 1972.

For a single day, the man in the white hat was as familiar to TV viewers as any Hollywood star. But this man was no movie actor. He was, in fact, the leader of an eight-man team on assignment for a little-known organization.

In the early-morning hours of September 5, 1972, the team scaled a fence and made its way into the Olympic Village in Munich, West Germany, where some 12,000 athletes from the more than 120 countries competing in the 17th Summer Games were housed. The men proceeded to Building 31, the apartment complex occupied by Israel's Olympic athletes. The man in the white hat knocked on the door. "Is this the Israeli team?" he asked.

The door was answered by Moshe Weinberg, the 32-year-old coach of the Israeli wrestling team. Weinberg opened the door a crack, saw a man holding a gun, and slammed the door shut. He yelled for the other athletes to escape.

Yosef Romano, a weight lifter, and Yosef Gitfreund, a wrestling referee, rushed to the door and helped Weinberg keep the intruders out. They were burly men, and the eight figures on the other side of the door were unable to push their way in.

"Boys, get out!" Gitfreund shouted to the athletes.

But the man in the white hat and his associates had automatic weapons. They shot through the door, killing Romano and Weinberg.

Some of the Israeli athletes did manage to escape. Gad Zavary, a boxer, broke through a window in his bedroom and jumped to safety. "They fired after me," Zavary said. "I heard bullets whistling by my ears."

Nine athletes weren't as lucky. They were taken hostage.

The man in the white hat and his seven companions, it turned out, were members of an organization calling itself Black September. They were terrorists.

✠   ✠   ✠

As the name suggests, terrorists try to terrorize, or strike fear into, a society or group of people. They do this by committing or threatening to commit acts of violence. In the end, they hope to achieve political goals, such as changing conditions in a society or even over-throwing a government.

In the case of the 1972 Olympics terrorism, the perpetrators had short- as well as long-term political goals. Their short-term goal was to force Israel and Germany to release 200 Palestinian prisoners they were holding. Black September's long-term goals were much more ambitious: the creation of a homeland for the Palestinian people—and indeed the total destruction of the nation of Israel.

Like the eight men who struck in Munich, terrorists are frequently members of groups, although they usually act alone or in small squads, called cells. This makes it more difficult for governments or law enforcement agencies to defeat the larger group: while the individual terrorist or terrorist cell may be captured or killed, the organization remains intact, and authorities can only guess at its precise structure and membership. Another reason terrorist organizations use attacks by individuals or small groups is that they can't directly confront the armed forces of their foes on the battlefield. They simply aren't large enough or powerful enough. In a traditional war against Israel, for example, Black September—indeed, all the terrorist groups fighting for a Palestinian homeland combined—would have been annihilated. For this reason it is often said that terrorism is a tool of the weak against the strong.

Terrorists may target governments, political parties, ethnic or religious groups, corporations, or even members of the news media. Sometimes they carry out political assassinations or murder specific individuals, but most often the violence is directed at random victims—for example, airline passengers on a given flight or anyone who happens to be in a certain place at a certain time. The randomness of an attack serves an important terrorist goal: bringing fear to, and undermining the sense of security of, large numbers of people, who realize that simply by virtue of being in the wrong place at the wrong time, they too could be victims. Indeed, terrorism is more about affecting the audience than about harming the actual victims. This is why terrorist groups often contact newspapers or TV stations and claim responsibility for their attacks, warning that similar acts of violence will be committed unless certain demands are met.

While the movies would have you believe that most terrorists are fanatical Arabs mixed up in the twisted and obscure politics of the Middle East, that is not true. Terrorism is a worldwide phenomenon, and even the United States, one of the most stable and secure countries, has experienced terrorism over the years. In the 1950s, for instance, two Puerto Rican terrorists tried to shoot their way into a house where President Harry Truman was living. Their goal was to kill the president and force the United States to grant independence to Puerto Rico. In the 1970s, a group of terrorists in California calling themselves the Symbionese Liberation Army murdered a school superintendent, kidnapped the daughter of a wealthy newspaper publisher, and robbed banks. And in 1995, in the worst terrorist attack ever on American soil, Timothy McVeigh used a truck bomb to destroy the Alfred P. Murrah Federal Building in Oklahoma City, killing 168 people. His apparent motive was to strike a blow against what he viewed as the tyranny of the federal government.

✠   ✠   ✠

The man in the white hat became familiar to millions of TV viewers worldwide because the Olympics were being covered by hundreds of reporters, including crews from international TV networks. In America, the ordeal was televised live by a sports crew that had been sent to Germany by the ABC television network. The crew was led by Jim McKay, the familiar host of ABC's *Wide World of Sports*.

"The sports events seemed like meaningless trivialities from another world as I watched them through the control room glass," McKay wrote in his autobiography, *The Real McKay*. "Glancing at my studio monitor, I felt I could almost touch the lookouts in front of Building 31—the young one in the hat, chain-smoking as he guarded the door, and the one in the ski mask, popping his head out a window like a character in some obscene

Punch and Judy show."

Whenever a Munich police negotiator approached the apartment building holding the terrorists and their hostages, he would be met on the balcony by the man in the white hat. The world would never learn the terrorist's name, but everyone who turned on a TV set that day would forever remember the image of the skinny man in the bucket-shaped white hat.

The world *would* learn the name of the group to which the man in the white hat belonged: Black September. The name referred to a particularly dark time in the decades-long Palestinian struggle to win a homeland.

In the late 1940s—when the new state of Israel defeated the attacking armies of Egypt, Iraq, Syria, Lebanon, and Jordan—nearly a million Arab Palestinians

For a few precious seconds, wrestling coach Moshe Weinberg and weight lifter Yosef Romano managed to keep the terrorists out of the Israeli apartment, allowing many of their teammates to escape. But the two men were eventually killed in this room in a hail of bullets.

were forced from their homes. Most of these people settled in crowded and impoverished refugee camps in Arab nations, dreaming of the day they would return to their original land.

In 1964, the Palestine Liberation Organization (PLO) was formed with the stated goal of destroying Israel and creating a Palestinian homeland. Eventually, it established headquarters in Jordan. Although the PLO had plenty of willing fighters, launching a war against Israel—the Middle East's most formidable military power—would have been suicidal. So the PLO contented itself with small-scale terrorist incursions into Israel. Because Israel made a practice of retaliating for terrorist attacks with air strikes on refugee camps and PLO bases within his borders, Jordan's King Hussein tried to restrain the PLO. As the years passed, however, the PLO grew entrenched in Jordan, becoming a virtual state within a state. Some Palestinian firebrands, impatient with the conservative approach of the PLO leadership and with the policies of their host, spoke of deposing King Hussein. Concerned that the stability of his own regime was threatened, Hussein launched a war to expel the PLO from his country in September 1970—Black September.

After a bitter defeat at the hands of the Jordanian army, the Palestinian cause was in shambles. But soon a more radical terrorist group, Black September, emerged with a new strategy: move the Palestinian fight onto the world stage. By 1972 the group—which claimed about 100 terrorist members, most living secretly in refugee camps in Jordan, Syria, Lebanon, and other Arab countries—had hit upon the perfect platform from which to publicize their struggle: the Summer Olympics.

The man in the white hat and his seven companions spent weeks hanging around Munich. They found jobs in the Olympic Village, learning where the Israeli athletes would be staying during the games.

The terrorists made their move at 4:20 A.M. on September 5. Maintenance workers saw the men, dressed in athletic warm-up suits, climbing over the fence but didn't think it unusual. Many of the athletes were known to go to after-hours parties and then find their way back to their rooms by climbing over the low and unguarded fence that surrounded the Olympic Village.

By dawn, Weinberg and Romano were dead and nine of their teammates were tied together, forced to sit on a bed under guard by the terrorists. German police surrounded Building 31. The man in the white hat emerged to deliver Black September's demands: release of the 200 Palestinian prisoners, and a plane to fly the terrorists from Germany to an Arab country of their choosing. If these demands weren't met, the man in the white hat said, his men would shoot two Israeli hostages at noon and two more at half-hour intervals thereafter.

Manfred Schreiber, the Munich police chief, met the Black September leader on the balcony. Later, Schreiber said that his first thought was to overpower the terrorist and take him captive.

"Do you want to take me?" the man in the white hat asked. He showed Schreiber that he held a hand grenade, and that his finger was on the pin.

Jim McKay recalled the scene as he watched on a TV monitor in the Olympic Village television studio, only a few hundred feet from Building 31. "All we saw on the screen," McKay revealed, "was the front of a building, the lookouts, and an occasional negotiator going in. There were no reports of an agreement. The picture was unchanging, yet the feeling of tension was growing, not only on the scene but, as we learned later, all across America. People stopped their working day to watch— in homes, offices, through appliance store windows."

The negotiations dragged on. Black September let its

noon deadline pass, and then let other deadlines pass as well. Finally, the Germans told Black September that their demands had been met: the Palestinian prisoners would be released. Also, an airplane would be provided for the terrorists' escape from Germany. What the terrorists didn't know was that the Israelis had steadfastly refused to release the prisoners—Israel had resolved never to bargain with terrorists—and that the Munich police intended to shoot the terrorists on the tarmac at the airport.

Willy Brandt, the German chancellor, claimed that his government never entertained the notion of letting the terrorists go. "That would be impossible for an honorable country to allow to happen," said Brandt. "We are responsible for the fate of these people."

At 10 P.M., nearly 18 hours after the terrorists had shot their way into the apartment in the Olympic Village, the Black September members led their hostages out of Building 31 and onto a bus provided by the German government. The bus was driven to an open field about 300 yards away, where two helicopters were waiting to fly the terrorists and hostages to an airport in Fürstenfeldbruck, about 16 miles away.

"The helicopters took off," wrote Jim McKay, "their little red identification lights blinking in the darkness. In the studio, we could feel the vibration as they clattered out of the village, only fifty feet or so over the heads of the crowd at the fence. Several thousand people were gathered in that crowd, staring up at the helicopters helplessly. Our daughter, Mary, was there and later said to me, 'Dad, they were so close that you felt you could almost touch them. Yet, no one could do anything to help them.'"

The flight to Fürstenfeldbruck took less than 30 minutes. The helicopters landed, and two of the terrorists got out to inspect the jet they believed would fly them out of the country.

At that point, things went terribly wrong. The Munich police had posted sharpshooters around the airport. According to the plan, when all eight terrorists stepped onto the tarmac, the sharpshooters were to pick them off. Inexplicably, though, the German police had deployed only five sharpshooters to take out eight terrorists. What's more, lighting on the tarmac was poor. The German army had offered the Munich police the use of infrared rifle scopes to help the sharpshooters see in the dark, but the police declined the offer because their men had never trained with the scopes.

The shooting started when only four of the terrorists had stepped onto the tarmac. Three of them were hit. The fourth—the man in the white hat—rolled under one of the helicopters and fired back, hitting spotlights that illuminated the tarmac. One of his bullets also struck

The burned-out shell of a helicopter stands in mute witness to the Munich police's failed attempt to rescue the Israeli hostages at the airfield in Fürstenfeldbruck. When police sharpshooters opened fire, one of the terrorists who was not hit tossed a grenade into the helicopter holding the hostages. All nine Israeli athletes perished.

The Olympic flame continues to burn, but the flags of the nations participating in the 17th Summer Games fly at half-mast in memory of the slain Israeli athletes.

and killed a Munich policeman.

The terrorists returned fire at the policemen, and as the gunfight raged, one of them tossed a grenade into the helicopter containing the hostages. All nine Israeli athletes were killed. Finally, after five of the terrorists were also killed, the remaining three surrendered. One of the dead terrorists was the leader—the man in the white hat. No one ever learned his name because he carried false identification.

Jim McKay recalled how he broke the news to the American public watching at home on TV: "Two of the hostages were killed in their rooms," McKay told millions of viewers. "Nine others were killed at the airport tonight." The sports anchor recalled that he felt tears well up in his eyes. "I tried to hold them back," he wrote. "I hoped my voice wouldn't break as I said the next three words: 'They're all gone.'"

There are more than a few footnotes to this story. Within hours of the Munich massacre, Israel retaliated, sending 75 air force jets into the skies over Syria and Lebanon to attack suspected terrorist bases. Sixty-six suspected terrorists were killed in the raids; dozens more were wounded. Three Syrian fighter jets were also shot down when they tried to repel the Israeli planes. Meanwhile, agents from the Mossad—Israel's intelligence service—fanned out across Europe and the Middle East and hunted down Black September leaders. In some cases, the relentless Mossad agents pursued the terrorists for years. In 1979—seven years after the Munich massacre—Mossad agents caught up with Ali Hassan Salemah, the organizer of the Olympic attack, and assassinated him by placing a bomb in his car. Essentially, Israel had decided to combat terror with terror.

And yet, after the Olympic massacre, Black September was far from finished. In 1973, Black September terrorists attacked an embassy in the Sudan, killing U.S. ambassador Cleo A. Noel and diplomats George Curtis Moore and Guy Eid. By 1974, world leaders refused to carry on diplomatic relations with the PLO—the group pursuing a Palestinian homeland—because of the terrorism practiced by Black September. So PLO chairman Yasir Arafat ordered Black September to disband. But that didn't mean an end to Palestinian terrorism. Black

In an eerie repeat of images from the Munich Olympics, hooded Black September terrorists stand on a terrace at the Saudi Arabian embassy in Khartoum, Sudan, March 3, 1973. During the Sudan incident the terrorists murdered three diplomats.

September's members joined other radical Palestinian groups and found new ways to commit terrorism. On June 24, 1976, seven terrorists—including five Palestinians—hijacked an Air France jet headed for Israel with 245 passengers aboard. The terrorists diverted the plane to Entebbe, Uganda, where soldiers of dictator Idi Amin would help guard the hostages. The terrorists demanded the release of 53 Palestinian prisoners held in Europe and Israel. They threatened to execute their hostages if the demands weren't met.

This time, the Israelis didn't place the fate of their hostages in the hands of another government. Instead, Israel dispatched a force of commandos, who stormed the Entebbe Airport and freed the hostages. Two passengers, all seven terrorists, and as many as 20 Ugandan soldiers, along with one Israeli officer, were killed in the commando raid.

The Palestinians eventually won their own homeland as Israel agreed to a phased withdrawal from the West Bank and Gaza Strip, territories that it had captured during wars with the Arab nations. The territories were administered on an interim basis by the Palestinian Authority, with the ultimate goal being the establishment of a permanent, independent Palestinian nation. However, it took years of diplomacy before the accords creating the Palestinian homeland were hammered out and signed on the White House lawn in 1995 by Israeli prime minister Yitzhak Rabin, PLO leader Yasir Arafat, and President Bill Clinton of the United States, and continued terrorism threatened to derail the plans for full Palestinian independence.

As for the three Olympic terrorists captured by the Munich police, within two months they were free men. Black September struck again, this time hijacking a German airliner and taking 13 passengers hostage. Their demand was the release of the three Munich terrorists. This time, rather than risk another airport shoot-out, the German authorities agreed to the exchange. The 13 airline passengers were released and the three terrorists were flown to Tripoli, the capital of Libya, where they were welcomed like conquering heroes.

Anarchy in America

2

"Lousy capitalists!" Guiseppe Zangara spat at witnesses as he was strapped into the electric chair. "No pictures! Capitalists! No one here to take my picture. All capitalists lousy bunch of crooks. Go ahead, push the button."

The executioner in the Florida State Penitentiary soon obliged, and Zangara's body was jolted with a fatal charge of electricity. He died at 9:17 A.M. on March 20, 1933, five weeks after firing shots into a car carrying President-elect Franklin D. Roosevelt and other dignitaries during a parade in Miami. Roosevelt was uninjured, but five people—including Anton Cermak, the mayor of Chicago—were wounded. Within days Cermak died from his wounds.

Police quickly identified Zangara as an anarchist—which, strictly speaking, refers to a person who opposes all organized authority but which in America typically meant a person, often a Communist, who advocated the use of violence to improve the plight of the working class. Anarchists generally identified both the government and capitalists as the enemies of working people. Although he acted alone, Zangara clearly had designs on bringing down the government of the United States.

"I don't like presidents and I would be glad if I had killed the president-elect," Zangara told police shortly after his arrest. He also told police that he hated rich people. (Roosevelt was a member of a prominent and wealthy family.)

Anarchism had swept across Europe in the troubled years following World War I—especially in Germany, where Communists and other political factions seeking to seize power fought pitched street battles with one another and the police. If Americans thought they were immune from the unrest, they couldn't have been more mistaken. In fact, anarchists were tossing bombs and bricks in American cities long before radical Communists took to the German streets in the 1920s. One incident that surely made Americans aware of the threat of anarchy was the assassination of President William McKinley on September 6, 1901.

McKinley's assassin, Leon Czolgosz, was born in Detroit, Michigan, to parents who had recently emigrated from Poland. Immigrants led hard lives in those days, and the Czolgosz family certainly struggled to make ends meet. In 1879, when Leon was six years old, he was forced to go to work shining shoes and selling newspapers to supplement his family's meager income. His mother died in 1885 during childbirth. At the age of 12, Leon had to work in a factory. By the time he was 16, he was working 12 hours a day in a glass factory for a

"I killed the president because he was the enemy of . . . the good working people," Leon Czolgosz said after assassinating President William McKinley at the 1901 Pan American Exposition in Buffalo, New York.

salary of about 75 cents a day.

"Czolgosz had to carry red hot glass from the ovens to the cooling racks. The heat was intense in such factories," wrote James W. Clarke in his book *American Assassins*. "Two suits of long woolen underwear were worn beneath an outer layer of clothing to provide some insulation from the searing temperatures. But even so, workers frequently developed severe abdominal pains and muscle cramps from dehydration. Bent over with pain, workers drank

Emma Goldman, an immigrant from Lithuania, became an anarchist in 1886 after police attempts to break up a union rally in Chicago led to the infamous Haymarket Riot.

salty pickle brine for relief."

Czolgosz and his family soon moved to Cleveland, Ohio, where Leon found work in a wire mill. Conditions were no better there. The work was dangerous: the wire often snapped, injuring or even killing workers. On one shift, Czolgosz narrowly escaped death when a snapped wire shot by his head. He sustained a nasty gash in his cheek, which left a scar. Later Czolgosz lost his job when he joined a union and went on strike for higher wages.

Elsewhere in America, poor conditions for workers spawned the labor movement. Unions slowly gained power in the early years of the 20th century, and eventually working conditions and wages improved. It was a long struggle that took years, and some people preached a much quicker solution for the worker's dilemma: anarchy.

One of the leaders of the anarchist movement at the turn of the century was Emma Goldman, an immigrant from Lithuania. Goldman became an anarchist in 1886 after 11 people were killed in Chicago's Haymarket Square during a union rally. As police moved to break up the peaceful rally, somebody tossed a bomb at them. The police responded by firing into the crowd. The incident became known as the Haymarket Riot.

The riot prompted Emma Goldman to start preaching the use of violence to support the cause of the worker. By 1901, she was editing an anarchist magazine and traveling the country, making speeches and encouraging people to take up the cause of anarchy.

Leon Czolgosz didn't need much encouragement. After losing his job in the wire factory, Czolgosz got himself rehired under a phony name. But he didn't hold the job for long. He soon lost interest in the wire mill as he found himself going to rallies where anarchists urged the use of violence against powerful industrialists and political leaders. In 1900, he attended a rally where Emma Goldman herself was the featured speaker.

Soon Czolgosz decided to kill President McKinley. He bought a gun at a local hardware store and traveled to Buffalo, New York, where McKinley planned to attend the Pan American Exposition, an event similar to a World's Fair. McKinley and his wife arrived at the exposition on September 4, 1901. Czolgosz followed the president around the grounds of the exposition for two days, waiting for his chance to get a good shot. Finally, on September 6, the president was shaking hands and talking with people in line at the Temple of Music. Czolgosz got into line. He took the gun out of his coat pocket and held it tightly in his hand, wrapping a handkerchief around it so that the president's guards could not see it. When the president reached out to shake his hand, Czolgosz drew his gun and fired. McKinley died in a hospital eight days later.

"I killed the president because he was the enemy of the good people—the good working people," Czolgosz said shortly after his arrest. "I am not sorry for my crime."

Czolgosz was convicted after a brief trial and executed on October 29, 1901. His death did nothing to stop the rise of anarchy in the United States. Emma Goldman and Alexander Berkman, another noted anarchist of the period, continued preaching violence as a means to obtain better conditions for working people.

Berkman was born in Vilna, Russia, the son of a prosperous family. While going to school in St. Petersburg, he was drawn to radical politics and the plight of the Russian peasant. But Russia in the 1880s was no place to question the authority of the powerful and autocratic czar. Berkman left Russia in 1887 and immigrated to the United States, where he continued his interest in radical politics. In 1892, during a strike by steelworkers, Berkman attempted to kill Henry Clay Frick, the manager of the Carnegie Steel Company. He was sentenced to 22 years in prison.

Prison failed to soften his resolve. After his release in 1914, Berkman joined forces with Goldman, helping her edit the anarchist magazine *Mother Earth* and later founding his own magazine, which he named *The Blast*.

In his first editorial, which appeared on January 15,

1916, Berkman spelled out the mission of his magazine in no uncertain terms:

> Do you mean to destroy?
>
> Do you mean to build?
>
> These are questions we have been asked from many quarters, by inquirers sympathetic and otherwise.
>
> Our reply is frank and bold:
>
> We mean both: to destroy and to build.
>
> For, socially speaking, Destruction is the beginning of Construction.
>
> Superficial minds speak sneeringly of destruction. Oh, it is easy to destroy—they say—but to build . . . to build . . . that's the important work.
>
> It's nonsense. No structure, social or otherwise, can endure if built on a foundation of lies. Before the garden can bloom, the weeds must be uprooted. Nothing is therefore more important than to destroy. Nothing more necessary and difficult.
>
> Take a man with an open mind, and you will have no great trouble in convincing him of the falsehood and rottenness of our social structure.
>
> But when one is filled with superstition and prejudice, your strongest arguments will knock in vain against the barred doors of his bigotry and ignorance. For thousand-year-old superstition and tradition is stronger than truth and logic.
>
> To destroy the Old and the False is the most vital work. We emphasize it: to blast the bulwarks of slavery and oppression is of primal necessity. It is the beginning of really lasting construction.
>
> Thus *The Blast* will be destructive.
>
> Thus *The Blast* will be constructive.

The language was meant to incite, but the first issues of *The Blast* had barely started smoldering in the hands of

Alexander Berkman at a 1914 funeral rally for workers killed during labor violence. Violence was at the heart of Berkman's prescription for reforming society. "Nothing is . . . more important than to destroy," the Russian-born anarchist once wrote.

American anarchists when the United States found itself at war in Europe. Emma Goldman, Alexander Berkman, and other leaders of the anarchist movement stayed on the stump, urging men to resist the draft, but their efforts largely fell on deaf ears. America enthusiastically entered World War I, which leaders characterized as a crusade "to make the world safe for democracy" and "the war to end all wars." The anarchists could do little but bide their time.

After the war, though, it didn't take long for the anarchists to resume their efforts. Late at night on June

2, 1919, a bomb exploded on the doorstep of Attorney General A. Mitchell Palmer. The bomb tore away much of the front of the attorney general's house. It also killed the hapless anarchist who had set the explosive.

Palmer and his family escaped unhurt, but the explosion shook the neighborhood. One of the neighbors stirred out of a sound sleep was the assistant secretary of the navy, who lived across the street. His name was Franklin D. Roosevelt, and 13 years later he would be elected president and survive an attempt on his own life by the anarchist Guiseppe Zangara.

It turned out that Palmer's house wasn't the only target of the anarchists. Eight other bombs were set off around Washington that night, causing damage to many buildings. At the site of each explosion, police found the same handwritten message: "The powers that be make no secret of their wills to stop world-wide spread of revolution. The powers that be must reckon that they will have to accept the fight they have provoked. A time has come when the social question's solution can be delayed no longer; class war is on and cannot cease but with a complete victory for the international proletariat."

To help achieve that victory, 38 other bombs were sent to government officials around the country, all of whom were known to be outspoken critics of the anarchist movement. Incredibly, nobody was killed.

Palmer acted quickly. He ordered the Justice Department's Bureau of Investigation—the forerunner of the Federal Bureau of Investigation, or FBI—to swoop down on the anarchists. One of the young federal agents drafted for the crackdown was J. Edgar Hoover, who would eventually become head of the FBI. In years to come, Hoover developed into a zealous Communist hunter, often violating the civil rights of thousands of innocent Americans in his relentless pursuit of "Reds."

This page: U.S. attorney general A. Mitchell Palmer, whose crackdown on anarchists—dubbed the "Red Raids"—pushed the envelope of constitutionality. Opposite page: Aftermath of the September 16, 1920, Wall Street bombing, an anarchist attack that claimed the lives of 38 persons and may have been in retaliation for Palmer's Red Raids.

But in the 1920s, law enforcement officials were hardly in a mood to care about the civil rights of suspected anarchists, many of whom were resident aliens who spoke little English and had no understanding of the Bill of Rights.

In 1920, Palmer wrote an essay titled "The Case Against the Reds." Here is how he explained his crackdown on the anarchists:

Like a prairie-fire, the blaze of revolution was sweeping over every American institution of law and order a

year ago. It was eating its way into the homes of the American workmen, its sharp tongues of revolutionary heat were licking the altars of the churches, leaping into the belfry of the school bell, crawling into the sacred corners of American homes, seeking to replace marriage vows with libertine laws, burning up the foundations of society.

Robbery, not war, is the ideal of communism. This has been demonstrated in Russia, Germany, and in America. As a foe, the anarchist is fearless of his own life, for his creed is a fanaticism that admits no respect of any other creed. Obviously it is the creed of any criminal mind, which reasons always from motives impossible to clean thought. Crime is the degenerate factor in society.

Upon these two basic certainties, first that the "Reds" were criminal aliens and secondly that the American Government must prevent crime, it was decided that there could be no nice distinctions drawn between the theoretical ideals of the radicals and their actual violations of our national laws. An assassin may have brilliant intellectuality, he may be able to excuse his murder or robbery with fine oratory, but any theory which excuses crime is not wanted in America. This is no place for the criminal to flourish, nor will he do so so long as the rights of common citizenship can be exerted to prevent him.

Palmer's raids—soon to be called the "Red Raids"—at first targeted members of the Federation of the Union of Russian Workers. Emma Goldman and Alexander Berkman were among the first to be arrested. J. Edgar Hoover personally prosecuted Goldman and Berkman, charging that Leon Czolgosz—the assassin of President McKinley—had learned the craft of anarchy from Goldman.

Although Berkman and Goldman could hardly be called innocent victims, many other people found they had few rights when the Red Raiders came crashing through their doors. Federal agents barged into homes without search warrants. They beat suspects and threw them into jails on the flimsiest of evidence. William J. Flynn, the head of the Bureau of Investigation, told his chief assistant, Frank Burke, that he had carte blanche in how he wished to treat the suspects. "I leave it entirely to your discretion as to the methods by which you should gain access to such places" to be raided, he told Burke.

Clearly the rights of innocent people were being violated. For example, in Connecticut a man was jailed for six months simply for expressing the opinion that Vladimir Lenin, who led the Bolshevik Revolution in Russia, was a man of intelligence. In Chicago a labor leader was nearly shot when he refused to stand at an outdoor concert while the national anthem was played. In all some 10,000 people were rounded up for questioning during the Red Raids.

The anarchists retaliated. On September 16, 1920, an anarchist drove a horse-drawn wagon onto Wall Street in the heart of the New York financial district. Quietly, the anarchist stepped off the wagon and walked away. Minutes later—just before noon—the wagon exploded. Obviously, it was the anarchist's intention to detonate the bomb as the noon lunch crowd flooded out of the office buildings that lined Wall Street. The explosion killed 38 innocent people and injured hundreds of others.

The government cracked down by ordering more raids. Hundreds of suspects were brought in for questioning and roughed up. Emma Goldman and Alexander Berkman were not among them. They had already been deported to Russia aboard the *Buford*, which set sail on December 21, 1919, with 247 anarchists aboard. All had been rounded up in the Red Raids and marched aboard the ship by a force of federal agents led by William J. Flynn.

Flynn personally walked Berkman up the gangplank of the ship. Once on deck, he turned to the anarchist and waved a finger in his face, telling him that if he ever returned to America he would spend the rest of his life in prison. Berkman glared back at Flynn.

"Don't be so glum," Flynn told him. "You're alive, aren't you?" Flynn suddenly withdrew a cigar and jammed it into the mouth of the startled Berkman. "You better enjoy that cigar, because you won't be getting any more where you're going," he said.

Flynn left the deck, and the *Buford* slowly pulled away. On the dock below, a crowd of dignitaries had gathered. "Merry Christmas, Emma!" someone shouted. Goldman would later write about that day aboard the ship in her autobiography, *Living My Life*:

> One by one the deportees marched [to the boat] flanked on each side by the uniformed men, curses and threats accompanying the thud of their feet on the frozen ground. When the last man had crossed the gangplank, the girls and I were ordered to follow, officers in front and in back of us.
>
> We were led to a cabin. A large fire roared in the iron stove filling the air with heat and fumes. There was no air nor water. Then came a violent lurch; we were on our way. I looked at my watch. It was 4:20 a.m. on the day of our Lord, December 21, 1919.
>
> On the deck above us I could hear the men tramping up and down in the wintry blast. I felt dizzy, visioning a transport of politicals doomed to Siberia. Russia of the past rose before me and I saw the revolutionary martyrs being driven into exile. But no, it was New York, it was America, the land of liberty! Through the port-hole I could see the great city receding into the distance, its sky-line of buildings traceable by their rearing heads. It was my beloved city, the metropolis of the New World. It was America, indeed America repeating the terrible scenes of czarist Russia! I glanced up—the Statue of Liberty!

As for Berkman, he intended to go out a bit more defiantly. As the ship started pulling away, Berkman shouted down toward Flynn: "We'll come back, and when we do, we'll get you."

But Alexander Berkman and Emma Goldman would not return. Berkman stayed in Russia for several years, then drifted around Europe, finally settling in Paris. He committed suicide there in 1936.

Goldman also left Russia and drifted around Europe. She died, little remembered, in 1940.

"Puerto Rico Is Not Free!"

Puerto Rican nationalists display the flag of their island, a commonwealth of the United States, during a demonstration near the Statue of Liberty. The movement for an independent Puerto Rico, which dates to the first decades of the 20th century, has inspired a significant amount of terrorism.

3

Oscar López Rivera sits in a federal prison. He has been incarcerated since 1980, and unless he wins an early parole it is likely he will die in prison. López Rivera's sentence expires in 2050, the year he turns 107.

To the U.S. Justice Department, Oscar López Rivera is prisoner 87651-024. He is an admitted terrorist.

"I have no regrets for what I've done in the Puerto Rico independence movement," says López Rivera. "Would I be willing to renounce the struggle for Puerto Rico's independence to get out of jail? I will never do that."

At the time of his arrest, López Rivera was a leader in the Fuerzas Armadas de Liberación Nacional—the Armed Forces of National Liberation—an organization best known by its acronym, FALN. During the

1970s and early 1980s, the FALN claimed responsibility for more than 100 bombings of public and commercial buildings in New York, Chicago, Washington, and Puerto Rico. In 1975, an FALN bomb killed 4 people and injured 60 more in Fraunces Tavern, a popular restaurant in New York. The colonnaded yellow-brick tavern, built in 1719, holds a place in American history as the site where George Washington announced his resignation as head of the army on December 4, 1783.

The FALN bomb exploded just before 1:30 P.M. on January 24, 1975, as a lunchtime crowd from New York's financial district filled Fraunces Tavern. Suddenly, dozens of windows shattered, doors splintered apart, interior walls crumbled, and a concrete and marble stairway collapsed. The powerful explosion shattered windows at the New York Telephone Company building across the street.

As alarms sounded, police cars, fire engines, and ambulance units raced through the crowded Lower Manhattan streets to reach the scene. Charles Anderson, a New York City firefighter, told the *New York Times*: "We saw people bleeding on the sidewalk, screaming in agony as we pulled up to the curb. It was utter havoc—people were lying all over the place, many of them mumbling in shock. Upstairs, some of the people were buried under debris. A lot of them were bleeding heavily from the face and the body."

An hour after the blast, FALN members called the Associated Press and United Press International news services and claimed responsibility for the attack. Police also found a typewritten note from the FALN in a telephone booth near the blast site.

"We, FALN, the Armed Forces of the Puerto Rican nation, take full responsibility for the especially detonated bomb that exploded today at Fraunces Tavern with

reactionary corporate executives inside," the note said. "The Yanki [American] government is trying to terrorize and kill our people to intimidate us from seeking our rightful independence from colonialism. They do this in the same way as they did in Vietnam, Guatemala, Chile, Argentina, Mexico, the Congo and in many other places, including the United States itself. . . . You have unleashed a storm from which you comfortable Yankis cannot escape. FREE PUERTO RICO RIGHT NOW!"

One of the victims of the Fraunces bombing was Frank Connor, a young New York City banker with a wife and two sons. He was killed by the bomb while eating lunch.

Historic Fraunces Tavern in New York City was the scene of a 1975 bombing by the Puerto Rican terrorist group FALN. The attack killed 4 and injured 60.

Oscar López Rivera, a leader of the FALN and an unrepentant terrorist, is serving a 70-year sentence.

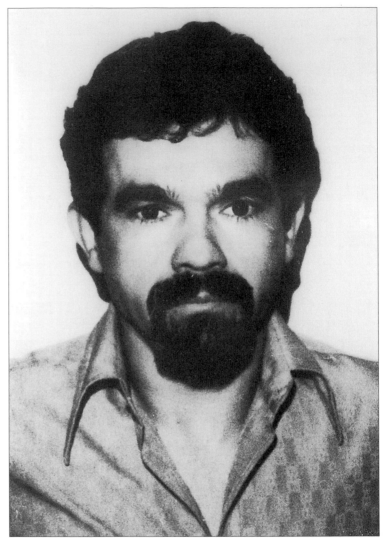

"He didn't have anything to do with Puerto Rico," says Joseph Connor, who was nine years old when his father died. "There is no correlation between Puerto Rican independence and blowing up innocent people in a restaurant."

López Rivera and 14 other FALN terrorists were arrested. Although not charged with taking part in specific bombings, the terrorists were accused of "seditious conspiracy to overthrow the government of the United

States in Puerto Rico by force."

López Rivera received one of the harsher terms. The judge sentenced him to serve 70 years in prison.

"I cannot undo what is done," shrugs López Rivera. "The whole thing of contrition, atonement—I have problems with that."

Puerto Rico is a commonwealth, a possession of the United States that is neither a state nor an independent nation. Christopher Columbus landed in Puerto Rico in 1493, and from then until the Spanish-American War in 1898 the Caribbean island was a colony of Spain. When Spain lost the war, it lost Puerto Rico to the United States.

Puerto Rico has its own government and constitution. Its people do not vote in American presidential elections, but they do send voting delegates to the Republican and Democratic national conventions, where the candidates for president are selected. Puerto Rico sends a member to the U.S. House of Representatives. That member has no vote, however, but merely voices the commonwealth's interests when Congress takes up issues that affect the island.

Puerto Rico's nearly four million residents have been, by and large, happy with their status over the years. Occasionally, a movement on the island favoring statehood or independence surfaces, but there is clearly no burning sentiment on the part of Puerto Ricans to become citizens of America's 51st state or an independent nation.

And yet, over the years, a core of *independistas* has continued to agitate for independence from the United States. That movement, which started shortly after World War I, was founded by a Harvard-educated lawyer from Puerto Rico named Pedro Albizu Campos. Albizu's resentment toward the United States stemmed from his service during World War I, when he claimed Puerto Ricans were not treated fairly by the U.S. Army.

After the war, Albizu joined the Nationalist Party in Puerto Rico. By 1930, he was the party's leader. He ran for a seat in the island's senate but managed to poll just 5,200 votes. From that point on, he decided that terrorism, not elective politics, would be the course followed by the National Party.

In 1932 Albizu led his followers on a march on the government headquarters in San Juan, the island's capital. The march soon turned violent, and one person was killed and a dozen injured.

Albizu's next move was to form the "Liberating Army of the Republic"—small units of armed men headquartered in towns surrounding San Juan. Albizu named himself commander in chief. Soon the Liberating Army of the Republic was ambushing island officials, including American diplomats stationed in Puerto Rico. In 1936, Albizu's followers assassinated Colonel Francis Riggs, a retired U.S. Army officer who headed the police on the island. Albizu and some of his followers were arrested, convicted of conspiracy in the Riggs murder, and imprisoned.

That didn't stop the independence movement. A year later, a parade staged by the Liberating Army in the town of Ponce touched off rioting that killed 6 people and injured 50 others. And in 1938, a colonel in the Puerto Rican National Guard was killed in a blast of terrorist gunfire.

By 1940, tensions between the United States and Germany and Japan were heating up. Congress authorized the Selective Service Administration to begin drafting American men to serve in the armed forces. Albizu—who was by now serving his prison sentence in a jail in Atlanta, Georgia—ordered his followers to refuse to register for the draft.

By 1950, Albizu was out of prison. It didn't take long for the violence to start again. In San Juan, the governor's house was attacked and a post office was set on fire. Bombs were thrown at police stations. In Jayuva, where some 15,000 Puerto Ricans lived, terrorists seized and held the town hall for 24 hours until troops showed up and routed them. Dozens of people were killed or wounded in the fighting.

In late October of 1950, two of Albizu's followers— Oscar Collazo and Griselio Torresola—made their way to Washington, D.C. Both men took hotel rooms, checking in with guns and ammunition hidden in their suitcases. Late in the afternoon of November 1, Collazo and Torresola unpacked their guns, hid them in their coat pockets, and took a taxi to Pennsylvania Avenue. Their intention was to kill President Harry Truman.

Presidents and their families normally live in the White House, but in 1950 the Executive Mansion was being renovated. So the Trumans had moved across the street to Blair House, a smaller mansion owned by the federal government and used mostly to house visiting heads of state and other dignitaries.

The Secret Service—the agency assigned to protect the president and his family—had been uncomfortable with the Trumans' decision to move into Blair House. The entrance to the home is virtually at street level, and unlike the White House, Blair House has no surrounding fence.

The Secret Service posted agents around the property and just inside the front door. Also stationed at the front door was a uniformed White House policeman. On November 1, 1950, Donald Birdzell was the officer assigned to guard the front door to Blair House.

Collazo and Torresola got out of the taxi just down the street from Blair House. It was a little past 2 P.M. Collazo approached the front door. Without saying a word, he drew his gun and tried to shoot Birdzell. But the gun misfired. Birdzell drew his gun but wasn't fast enough.

Collazo fired again, discharging all eight shots at the policeman. Birdzell was hit, but as he collapsed to the sidewalk he managed to get off a shot at Collazo, who was struck in the chest.

Two other policemen—Joseph Downs and Leslie Coffelt—heard the shots and came to Birdzell's aid. They didn't see Torresola, who had slipped into some bushes in front of Blair House. Torresola shot at the two men, hitting both of them. As he fell to the ground Coffelt fired back and killed Torresola.

By now, sirens were shrieking and more policemen and Secret Service agents were rushing to the scene. In two minutes, 27 shots had been fired, breaking the peace on what had been a lazy autumn afternoon in Washington.

Upstairs in Blair House, the president had just awakened from an afternoon nap. Dressed in his underwear, he had heard the shots and leaned out his bedroom window to see what was going on. The first lady, Bess Truman, also leaned out the window.

"Harry!" she gasped. "Someone is shooting our policemen."

A Secret Service agent saw the Trumans leaning out the window. "Get back!" he shouted. "Get back!"

The incident was over quickly. Collazo and Torresola never made it past the front steps of Blair House.

There was no question who had ordered the terrorist attack on the president. In Torresola's pocket, investigators found a note from Albizu, wishing the terrorist luck in his attack on the president.

"Dear Griselio," the note said, "if for any reason it should be necessary for you to assume the leadership of the movement in the United States, you will do so without hesitation of any kind. We are leaving to your high sense of patriotism and sane judgment everything regard-

ing this matter. Cordially yours, Pedro Albizu Campos."

Collazo, still alive, was rushed to Gallinger Hospital in Washington, where he was treated for his chest wound. He admitted to investigators that he intended to kill the president. He was tried for the murder of Officer Leslie Coffelt, who had died from his wounds. Collazo was convicted and sentenced to death in the electric chair, but in 1952 President Truman commuted his sentence to life imprisonment.

As for President Truman, shortly after the shooting he hurried off to Arlington National Cemetery, where he kept an appointment to speak at the dedication of a statue of World War II hero John Dill. "A president has to

A Secret Service agent stands over the prone body of Oscar Collazo, one of two Puerto Rican nationalists who tried to shoot their way into Blair House in Washington, D.C., to assassinate President Harry S. Truman. Collazo survived a chest wound, but his partner and a White House policeman died in the attack.

expect these things," he shrugged to reporters, who questioned him about the shooting when he arrived to make the speech.

Ironically, Albizu and his followers had nothing to gain from the murder of President Truman. Indeed, Truman had convinced Congress to let the people of Puerto Rico elect their own governor and create their own constitution—both important steps toward an independent Puerto Rico.

"The Puerto Rican people should have the right to determine for themselves Puerto Rico's political relationship to the United States," Truman said in a speech in San Juan in 1948. Clearly, Harry Truman would not have stood in the way of a legal movement toward independence by the people of Puerto Rico.

Even though they had botched the assassination attempt on President Truman, the *independistas* were not through. The floor of the U.S. House of Representatives in the Capitol would be the scene of another terrorist incident. It was March 1, 1954. Nearly 250 members of Congress gathered on the House floor for routine business. At the entrance to the Visitors Gallery in the Capitol, two men and a woman approached W. Swem Elgin, the doorkeeper. They asked if they might sit in the gallery to watch the House debate.

"You got any cameras?" Elgin asked. (Flash photography is strictly forbidden in the Capitol.)

No, they told Elgin, they carried no cameras.

One of the three people who approached Elgin was Rafael Miranda, an Albizu follower who had served one year in jail for dodging the draft. The others were Andrés Figueroa Cordero and Lolita Lebron. Elgin motioned for them to enter the gallery.

Miranda and the others found seats in the back row. On the floor, House Speaker Joe Martin was counting

votes on an immigration bill. Suddenly, the three visitors whipped out automatic pistols.

"Puerto Rico is not free!" shouted Lolita Lebron.

Then the shooting started. Miranda, Cordero, and Lebron opened fire, spraying the House chamber with bullets. Chaos broke out around them. On the floor, some congressmen stood frozen in terror while others dived for cover. Alarms were sounded. Tourists in the Visitors Gallery huddled together, frightened that the two men and the woman would turn their guns on them. Nevertheless, the shooting was over in seconds. Police rushed to the scene and subdued the terrorists as they were trying to escape, but not before five congressmen—

President Truman in the Oval Office. From a strategic standpoint, the Puerto Rican terrorists' decision to assassinate the president made little sense, as Truman had previously stated his belief that the Puerto Rican people should have the right to determine their political future.

In police custody after their attack on the U.S. House of Representatives wounded five congressmen are, from right, Andrés Figueroa Cordero, Lolita Lebron, and Rafael Miranda. At left is fellow Puerto Rican nationalist Irving Flores, who at the last minute decided not to participate in the shooting.

Alvin Bentley of Michigan, Ben Franklin Jensen of Iowa, Clifford Davis of Tennessee, George Fallon of Maryland, and Kenneth Roberts of Alabama—were hit by gunfire. Luckily, none of their wounds proved fatal.

The three terrorists were quickly hustled off to jail. A fourth terrorist, who had decided not to go through with the plot, was picked up at a bus terminal. The four had arrived in Washington that day from New York on one-way train tickets. Apparently, all four believed they would not live to see the next day.

Police found a note in Lolita Lebron's handbag. It read: "Before God, and the world, my blood claims for the independence of Puerto Rico. My life I give for the freedom of my country. This is a cry for victory in our struggle for independence."

Certainly, whatever sentiment members of Congress might have had for an independent Puerto Rico disappeared as the three terrorists sprayed the chamber with gunfire. But over the years, the question of statehood or independence for Puerto Rico has repeatedly found its way to Congress. On the island, the people have voted in referenda. The matter has been debated in political elections and argued across tabletops in San Juan's cantinas. And it has never been settled.

In 1993, Puerto Ricans voted on whether to petition Congress for statehood or independence. Statehood failed to receive a majority. Independence did far worse, garnering only 4 percent of the vote. In December 1998 another plebiscite was held to determine Puerto Ricans' wishes for their future political status. Amid suggestions that the ramifications of the options weren't explained clearly enough, "none of the above" beat out statehood and independence. And so Puerto Rico remains a commonwealth.

As for Pedro Albizu Campos, following the shooting in the Capitol he was tracked down in Puerto Rico, where he was arrested and returned to jail. In 1956, he suffered a stroke and was never the firebrand again. Pardoned in 1964, he died the following year, never seeing an independent Puerto Rico.

Although Oscar López Rivera keeps the faith, other FALN members are unsure of their previous terrorist tactics. In 1995, Alberto Rodríguez, one of the terrorists arrested with López Rivera, asked the parole board to release him, claiming that he had changed his mind about how to achieve Puerto Rico's independence. In a statement to the parole board, Rodríguez wrote:

I now recognize that many of the assumptions that guided my actions over 12 years ago were simply wrong. I sincerely believed that the majority of Puerto Ricans desired independence from the United States, and that the only thing keeping the island from achieving its independence was the power of the United States government. I also believed that all legal avenues for seeking independence were exhausted, or closed. . . .

I raise this now because it is important for the parole board to understand why I committed my offenses. I was motivated by ideas, not greed, power, emotions, love of violence, or by some romantic notion of being a heroic freedom fighter. I love my country and want to see it an independent nation, but I now recognize that this is a question to be resolved politically, not violently.

Rodríguez was denied parole, but in 1999 President Bill Clinton granted clemency to him and 11 other FALN members, ordering their releases from what had been lengthy prison terms. In return, the former terrorists agreed to renounce the use of violence to achieve independence for Puerto Rico. Oscar López Rivera and another FALN member, Antonio Camacho-Negron, turned down the clemency offer and remain in prison.

The terrorists who stormed the U.S. House of Representatives in 1954 were sentenced to lengthy prison terms. In 1975, their names were listed in the FALN letter found by police following the Fraunces Tavern bombing. The FALN threatened other acts of terror unless they were released from prison. The government refused, but in 1979 they too were granted clemency by President Jimmy Carter, who thought they had served long enough. Carter also released Oscar Collazo, who had tried to shoot his way into Blair House. They all slipped quietly back to Puerto Rico, although Lolita Lebron has continued her activism nonviolently over the years. In 1997, she returned to New York to testify before a United Nations committee studying decolonization.

Puerto Rico, she told the U.N. panel, "is a nation with a beautiful fighting tradition that dates back many centuries. It is precisely this that guarantees the defeat of colonialism and our place in history as a free people."

Tania

If you were a student at the University of California at Berkeley in the early 1970s, you might have stopped by the Fruity Rudy juice stand on the outskirts of the campus and enjoyed a freshly squeezed glass of fruit juice. The Fruity Rudy stand was painted orange and had a green awning, but by no means did it stand out from the other colorful kiosks and food stands that lined Telegraph Avenue.

A young woman worked in the stand, squeezing juice for customers. Her name was Nancy Ling Perry. A tiny woman standing just 4 feet 11 inches tall, she held a degree in English and was taking graduate courses in chemistry. But Nancy Ling Perry didn't intend to teach English or become a chemist. And she certainly didn't intend to squeeze juice in the Fruity Rudy stand for the rest of her life.

Nancy Ling Perry considered herself a revolutionary. She aimed to overthrow the government of the United States, and she was prepared to take up arms to do so. She had already joined a bizarre group of ex-convicts, college students, and others who made up an organization they had named the Symbionese Liberation Army (SLA). When she wasn't working at the fruit stand or taking classes at Berkeley, Nancy Ling Perry was collecting guns, learning guerrilla tactics, and drafting the manifesto that would set down the SLA's plan for assassinations, robberies, and kidnappings.

Every member of the SLA had to adopt a new name. "My name was Nancy Ling Perry but my true name is Fahizah," Perry wrote. "I have learned that what one really believes in is what will come to pass."

✠   ✠   ✠

San Francisco in the 1960s was a place where you could find hippies and flower power, psychedelic music and psychedelic drugs. The rock band Jefferson Airplane got its start at a hip San Francisco club named the Matrix. In 1967, the Summer of Love was in full bloom in San Francisco. In the Haight-Ashbury district, a visitor might be stopped and asked for some spare change or, failing that, spare dope.

Across the San Francisco Bay is the community of Berkeley, home of the University of California campus at Berkeley. Radical politics were very much in vogue at Berkeley in the 1960s. In 1964, students at Berkeley rose up in protest when the college administration refused to allow them to set up tables at the entrance to the campus to distribute literature and collect donations to support candidates for office and trumpet other causes, such as the civil rights movement. The students believed the university's edict violated their First Amendment rights of free speech. They blocked the entrance to Sproul Hall, the administration building, and forced university administrators to give them their rights to free expression. Their protest came to be known as the Free Speech Movement, or FSM.

The FSM was merely a precursor of what was to come. Soon Berkeley became the center of the protest movement against the Vietnam War. In 1965, student activist Jerry Rubin led some 500 Berkeley students to a nearby railroad station, where they sat on the tracks, boarded an army troop train en route to Oakland, and passed out antiwar leaflets to draftees.

"The lid was coming off," wrote David Goines, one of the students who organized the FSM. "Things were going to get a whole lot worse by the end of the decade."

Things did get worse. Student protests against the war helped convince President Lyndon Johnson not to seek reelection in 1968. At the Democratic National Convention in Chicago that year, violent clashes broke out between antiwar demonstrators and the police. At Kent State University in Ohio, four students died in 1970 when National Guardsmen fired into a crowd of protesters.

By the early 1970s, America had gotten out of the war and the students had gone back to their classrooms. But in the neighborhoods surrounding the Berkeley campus, people still marched to the beat of a different drum. Strolling through the Berkeley neighborhoods, you might see kiosks adorned with advertisements for psychic healing, acupuncture, meditation, kung fu, red pepper cures, and dream control.

But beneath this calm, funky exterior, a cult of terrorists had organized themselves and made ready their plans for the violent overthrow of society. They were led by an escaped prison inmate named Donald David DeFreeze, who gave himself the rank of general field

"Soldiers" of the SLA. From left: Donald DeFreeze, aka Field Marshal Cinque; William Wolfe; Camilla Hall. All would die in a shoot-out with police and the FBI.

marshal. Seven other "soldiers" signed on to join DeFreeze. They called themselves the Symbionese Liberation Army—the term *Symbionese* meaning, according to its members, the "body of harmony of dissimilar bodies and organisms living deep and within the body."

The SLA preached radical left-wing politics. The members read books written by Karl Marx, the founder of international communism, and Eldridge Cleaver, the American Black Power leader. They believed the gap between rich and poor had grown too large. They gathered weapons and learned how to use them. They dropped their names and adopted new ones. DeFreeze became Cinque. William Wolfe became Cujo. Patricia Soltysik took the name Mizmoon. William Harris became Teko, while his wife, Emily, took the name Yolanda. As a symbol, they chose a drawing of a coiled, seven-headed cobra.

"The Symbionese Liberation Army has selected the seven-headed cobra as our emblem because we realize that an army is a mass that needs unity in order to become a fighting force, and we know the true unity among people must be based on a concern that is universal," the SLA said in its manifesto. "It is a revolutionary unity of all people against a common oppressor enemy of the people. This unity of seven heads in one body defines the essence of cooperation and socialism in the great undertaking of revolutionary war."

The SLA's first target was Marcus Foster, the superintendent of schools of Oakland, who had proposed to his city's school board that all students be photographed and issued identification cards. Foster also wanted to post guards in the schools. On November 6, 1973, Foster was shot to death by SLA members.

Less than three months later, a van containing two SLA members, Russell Little and Joseph Remiro, was pulled over by police in Concord, California, for a routine traffic stop. Remiro and Little jumped out of the van, drawing guns and opening fire on the police. In the gun battle that ensued, Little was wounded and captured. Remiro initially got away but was eventually taken into custody.

When police announced they would charge Remiro and Little with Marcus Foster's murder, Nancy Ling Perry sent a letter to the authorities announcing that the two terrorists were members of the Symbionese Liberation Army. Ling's letter said: "The action taken by the SLA combat unit in reference to the Oakland Board of Education was a specific response to political police state programs and the failure of the Board to heed the rights and demands of the people in the community. The specific program was one of the photo identification (similar to the system of apartheid in South Africa), biological classification in the form of bio-dossiers which classify students according to race and political beliefs, internal warfare computer files, and armed police state patrols within the schools."

Showing signs of the beating he received from the SLA members who kidnapped his fiancée, Steven Weed speaks with reporters. At left is Catherine Hearst, Patty's mother.

Ling also warned police that they would be up against a campaign of terror:

Beginning January 11, a directive was issued by the SLA and the Court of the People stating that as of that date, all units of the Symbionese Liberation Army are to be heavily and offensively armed with cyanide bullets in all their weapons. I would like to convey the word to [Remiro and Little]: you have not been forgotten, and you will be defended because there has been no set back and all combat forces are intact. There really are no words available to me to express what I feel about the capture of [Remiro and Little]. They are in a concentration camp now because none of us were offensively armed, and because I was not aware that they were under attack. But my beautiful brothers, as we have said many times, we learn from our mistakes, and we learn from our active participation in struggle, not from political rhetoric, so we won't cry, but simply fight on; and right on with that. DEATH TO THE FASCIST INSECT THAT PREYS UPON THE LIFE OF THE PEOPLE.

The letter was signed "Fahizah."

At the time of their arrests, the van driven by Remiro and Little had been stopped within a few blocks of a house where the SLA was making bombs and storing arms. A few days after the arrest, Perry set fire to the house and burned it down. When investigators sifted through the wreckage, they found this note: "Patricia Campbell Hearst on the night of the full moon."

✠   ✠   ✠

Patty Hearst was the daughter of wealthy newspaper publisher Randolph Hearst and the granddaughter of William Randolph Hearst, who had founded his family's media empire and was one of the nation's richest and most powerful men during the first half of the 20th century. William Randolph Hearst built San Simeon, an enormous castle filled with rare works of art, oriental rugs, artifacts, books, and other treasures on 285,000 acres of lush California forest about midway between Los Angeles and San Francisco. Today, San Simeon is owned by the state of California, which maintains it as a museum. But in William Randolph Hearst's day, it was a center of power—a place where Hearst would entertain political figures, Hollywood stars, and international heads of state.

Patty Hearst did not grow up in San Simeon, but she never wanted for anything. As a young girl, her home was a 22-room mansion with Greek columns on Santa Ynez Avenue in Hillsborough, a fashionable San Francisco suburb. Patty went to private schools, learned how to ride horses, drove a sports car, and traveled in Europe. As the student protests erupted on the nearby Berkeley campus, she paid them little mind.

She also fell in love with her math teacher, Steven Weed. He was 23; Patty, 17. By the time Patty Hearst turned 18, she was living with him. When Steven won a fellowship to teach and study at Berkeley, Patty decided to go with him. They left Hillsborough and moved into a small apartment on Benvenue Street in Berkeley, just a few blocks from the campus. Patty took classes at Berkeley as well. They settled into their new lives, making plans to marry.

On February 1, 1974, Patty answered the ring of the apartment's doorbell. A tall young woman stood at the threshold. She asked Patty whether the apartment was for rent. Patty told her no, it wasn't. Just as the young woman turned to leave, Patty noticed that a man had accompanied her and that she thought the man had acted "nervously, wringing his gloved hands and glancing from side to side."

In her autobiography, *Every Secret Thing*, Patty would write: "We laughed them off as Berkeley weirdos, yet I just did not think that they were really apartment hunting. For the next couple of days I could not shake off this heavy, oppressive feeling that something was not right, that something bad was going to happen either to me or to someone I loved. I had no idea what it might be

The SLA demanded that Randolph Hearst give away $6 million in food to the poor. As this photo shows, however, the distribution was extremely disorganized, and the program soon fell apart.

or why I felt this way."

Three days later, Patty found out. At 9 P.M. on February 4, 1974, Patty and Steven were at home, relaxing in front of the TV, when the doorbell rang. Patty looked up as her fiancé went to open the door.

"I could see the bulky outline of a person standing beyond the frosted sliding glass door," Patty wrote.

"That looks weird," I said. Feeling jumpy, I thought of warning Steve to put the chain on the door before he unlocked it, but he didn't give me a chance. By that time he had the door open and I had walked into the narrow hallway, a few feet behind him, wondering what was up. I could hear a girl's agitated voice. Her words came tum-

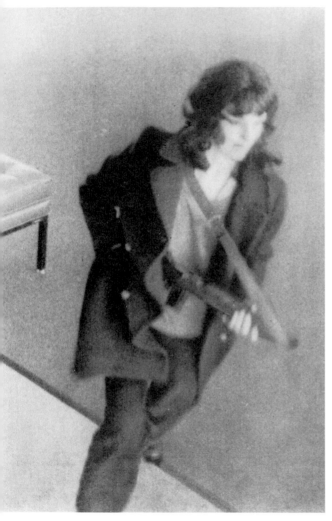

A surveillance camera captured this image of Patty Hearst cradling a carbine during an SLA robbery of the Hibernia National Bank in San Francisco—stunning evidence that the captive had joined her captors.

bling out so fast that I could barely make out what she was saying. . . . At that moment I heard a scuffling commotion and turned to see two men with guns burst into the apartment. . . . I backed away from them into the kitchen, shocked, screaming. Then the girl came after me, backing me into the stove, pointing a black automatic pistol in my face. At the same time, she clamped her hand over my mouth and said, "Be quiet and nobody will get hurt."

The assailants threw Patty to the floor, tied her up, and blindfolded her. They beat Steven violently. Patty started screaming. She was dragged out of the house and struck with a rifle butt to quiet her. She was thrown into the trunk of a car and driven to a house in Daly City near San Francisco, where her captors locked her in a closet.

The SLA members had big plans for their hostage. They intended to offer her in a prisoner trade for Remiro and Little. They also wanted her father to put up millions of dollars to fund a food giveaway program for the poor. On February 12, eight days after the kidnapping, Patty Hearst recorded a tape that the SLA sent to police.

"I just want to get out of here and see everyone again and be back with Steve," Patty said on the tape. "I just hope you'll do whatever they say, Dad, and just do it quickly."

Randolph Hearst offered to put up $2 million for the food program. The SLA demanded $4 million more, but Hearst claimed he didn't have the money. Weeks went by. On March 4, Patty made another tape: "I don't think you're doing everything you can, everything in your power. I don't believe you're doing anything at all," she complained. "You said it was out of your hands; what you should have said was that you wash your hands of it. If it had been you, Mom, or you, Dad, who had been kidnapped instead of me, I know that I and the rest of the family would have done anything to get you back. I'm starting to think no one is concerned about me anymore."

Randolph Hearst was able to raise the rest of the money when his corporation donated $4 million to the food program. Hundreds of people in California received parcels of food, but the distribution was haphazard and poorly managed and the program soon fell apart. Certainly, the SLA's tactics hardly had a positive long-term impact on the lives of poor Californians.

Meanwhile, something was happening to Patty: she was coming to identify with her captors. Experts in the dynamics of hostage situations know that this phenomenon—known as the Stockholm syndrome—isn't at all unusual. Because a hostage's life is at the whim of her captors, subconsciously she will try to believe in their basic goodness. But the SLA was also actively brainwashing Patty, making her believe in their cause. By keeping her locked in a closet, by constantly berating her as a wealthy young woman with no feelings for poor people, by barraging her with a steady diet of revolutionary rhetoric, the SLA members succeeded in turning Patty Hearst into a soldier of the Symbionese Liberation Army.

On April 4, Patty recorded another tape. On it she announced that she had joined the SLA and accused her parents of stalling for time so that the FBI could track her down and murder her.

"Your actions have taught me a great lesson," she told her parents on the tape. "In a strange kind of way I'm

Los Angeles police officers take cover behind cars as the SLA's house on East 54th Street burns. During the hour-long gun battle that culminated in the blaze, police and FBI agents had fired some 6,000 rounds of ammunition. Five SLA members died in the shoot-out and fire.

grateful to you."

Patty took the name Tania. She posed for a photograph in front of a banner of the seven-headed cobra. On April 15, Patty Hearst, cradling a carbine, marched into the Hibernia National Bank in San Francisco and participated in a daring daylight robbery of the bank with other members of the SLA.

"I don't remember saying or doing anything other than point my carbine at the people on the floor in front of me," Patty later wrote. "The assistant manager said later that he had asked me where he should lie down and that I did not respond. On his own, he joined the others who were bunched together in a group on the floor, belly down, glancing up at me."

The SLA headed south to Inglewood, near Los

Angeles, where Patty and William and Emily Harris robbed a sporting goods store, spraying the building with bullets. Three days later, on May 17, 1974, police received a tip that the SLA was hiding at a house on East 54th Street in Los Angeles. More than 400 police officers and FBI agents surrounded the house.

A gunfight started. In just one hour, more than 6,000 shots were fired. The house caught fire and burned down. In the rubble, police found the bodies of five SLA members, including Donald DeFreeze and Nancy Ling Perry. At large still were four others: William and Emily Harris, Wendy Yoshimura, and Patty Hearst.

The remaining members of the SLA were on the run for more than a year. During that time, they crossed the country, spending time near Scranton, Pennsylvania, and on an abandoned dairy farm in New York's Catskill Mountains. Even on the run, with most of their members dead, the remaining SLA "soldiers" still believed in the revolution. William Harris, known as Teko, had taken over command now that Cinque was dead.

"At the dairy farm we went on with our calisthenics and combat drills, but this time Teko devised a new method of torturing us into condition," Patty wrote.

> He instituted practice guerilla-warfare maneuvers, staging mock search-and-destroy missions by dividing us into two teams: the pursued and the pursuers. If Wendy and I were the team to be pursued, we would be given a three-minute head start. We would have to run like mad up the hills, through the woods beyond the house, across a dirt road, through a field and up another hill, and through even more fields. Our goal was a stone wall about two miles from the farmhouse. Or we could stop and hide at some point in the woods and try to ambush our pursuers. When we were the

pursuers, chasing Teko and Yolanda, we could proceed as fast or as slowly as we wished, although on the alert for an ambush, but the object was to catch up to and either capture or kill the other team.

Eventually the group decided to return to California. They found an apartment on Morse Street in San Francisco. They started drafting new members of the SLA and talked of leaving San Francisco for Oregon or Massachusetts. One afternoon in late September 1975, Patty Hearst and Wendy Yoshimura were sitting at the kitchen table in the Morse Street apartment when they heard a short and loud command: "Freeze! FBI . . . Freeze!"

Patty and Wendy were arrested. The police had also tracked down the Harrises.

When Patty Hearst was booked at the jail, she was asked her occupation. "Urban guerrilla," she said.

William and Emily Harris were charged with the kidnapping of Patty Hearst. They were convicted and sentenced to lengthy prison terms but paroled in 1983. In June 1977, Joseph Remiro and Russell Little were convicted in the murder of Marcus Foster, the Oakland school superintendent. They were sentenced to life in prison.

Patty Hearst was charged with participating in the robbery of the Hibernia National Bank. She was sentenced to seven years in prison but served only two years before her sentence was commuted by President Jimmy Carter.

As for Steven Weed, his relationship with Patty Hearst was over. He remains one of the truly tragic figures in the SLA saga.

Years later, Steven would write: "Just now, thinking back to our days in Berkeley, I remember walking to campus one afternoon and seeing her coming toward me, the same, choppy, determined little step bouncing her

Patty Hearst is led into court. Despite the mental and physical abuse her captors had inflicted, a jury convicted Hearst of taking part in the Hibernia bank robbery. She served two years in prison before President Jimmy Carter commuted her seven-year sentence.

along. Her face was downcast, preoccupied with thoughts about a paper due, perhaps, or another book to read. She didn't see me leaning against a tree, watching her, smiling at her. Then, when she was only a few steps away, she looked up and there was this wide smile, half-surprised, half-self mocking, her hands stretching out as if to say, 'You caught me. Here I am.'"

The *Fatwa*

Kafr al-Dawar is hardly anyone's idea of paradise. Located in the Nile Delta in northern Egypt, the city's 250,000 people live in close quarters. Most people reside in tiny apartments stacked on top of one another in featureless concrete bungalows. The streets are unpaved. Unemployment is high. People who do have jobs work long hours in dank and depressing factories. The police and the government of President Hosni Mubarak are despised. Graffiti artists run rampant through Kafr, spraying messages and slogans on the walls of buildings. A typical message: Islam is the Solution.

Mahmud Abouhalima was born in Kafr in 1959. As a young man, he embraced the tenets of Islam and grew to hate the Western influences that, he felt, were coming to dominate his country. He was certainly not alone in

73

Egyptian-born Mahmud Abouhalima fled his native country after police began rounding up fellow Muslim fundamentalists. He eventually settled in New York.

this feeling. In Iran in 1978, fundamentalist Muslims led by the exiled Ayatollah Ruhollah Khomeini overthrew the government of the American-backed Shah Mohammad Reza Pahlavi. A year later, fanatical students taking their orders from Khomeini broke into the U.S. embassy in Tehran and took hostage 63 embassy workers, holding them for more than a year. The students demanded the return of the shah, a condition that would never be met. Nevertheless, the message to the Western world was clear: fundamentalist Islamic militancy was sweeping through the Middle East, and leaders of the movement aimed to rid Arab countries of all Western influence.

Back in Kafr, Abouhalima had joined al-Jama'a Islamiyya, an outlawed organization that was committed to making Egypt a fundamentalist Islamic state. But Egypt's president, Anwar Sadat, aimed to stamp out the fundamentalist movement before it swept through his country, as it had in Iran. He ordered arrests of fundamentalist leaders, including members of al-Jama'a Islamiyya. Some 2,000 Egyptians, including many of Abouhalima's friends, were rounded up and thrown into prisons. Realizing that government agents were on his trail as well, Abouhalima fled Egypt and made his way to Germany.

On October 6, 1981—one week after Abouhalima arrived in Germany—Anwar Sadat stood reviewing the troops of the Egyptian army. No Arab leader had done more to modernize his country and invite trade with the West than Sadat. What's more, Sadat was the first Arab leader to sign a peace treaty with Israel, which was almost universally hated by the Arab states.

As Sadat inspected the ranks of his soldiers, a military truck drove up and stopped suddenly only a few feet from the president. Four soldiers leaped out of the truck and started firing at the president.

"I am Khalid al-Islambouli," one of the attackers shouted. "I have killed Pharaoh!"

The men were quickly subdued, but not before Sadat had sustained fatal wounds. The four soldiers as well as another man were quickly tried and executed for the attack.

One other man was also arrested and charged with issuing a *fatwa*, or Islamic religious decree, ordering the assassination. That man was Sheik Omar Abdel Rahman. Rahman would eventually be found not guilty of

"Hit hard and kill the enemies of God," Sheik Omar Abdel Rahman, a blind Muslim cleric, exhorted his followers. Rahman was at the center of plots to blow up the World Trade Center and a handful of other New York City landmarks.

issuing the fatwa, but the government made it clear that it wanted him out of the country. So Rahman made his way south to Sudan, and from there he traveled to the United States.

After leaving Egypt, Abouhalima spent the next four years in Germany. He married, divorced, and remarried. His second wife, a German, converted to Islam. In 1985, Abouhalima and his wife left Germany and headed for the United States, arriving in New York. Abouhalima became a taxi driver. The couple appeared to settle into the lives of typical young New Yorkers.

But Abouhalima would be drawn to a conflict raging halfway around the world. Years before, in 1979, the army of the Soviet Union had invaded the Muslim nation of Afghanistan. Muslims everywhere were horrified. The Soviet Union was a country founded on the principles of communism. One of its main principles was state-sponsored atheism, the belief that no god exists. What's more, religious leaders throughout the Soviet Union were persecuted. In Afghanistan, Muslim resistance fighters, known as *mujahedin*, took to the rugged mountains, using guerrilla tactics to battle the Soviet Union's modern tanks and helicopters. The Soviet soldiers and mujahedin settled in for a long, bloody guerrilla war.

As he drove his taxi, Abouhalima dreamed of participating in the *jihad*, or holy war, in Afghanistan. Muslims from around the world were traveling to Afghanistan to fight alongside the mujahedin. In late 1988, Abouhalima left New York to participate in the jihad.

He spent 20 months in Afghanistan, receiving combat training and fighting with the mujahedin. By 1989, the Soviets had had enough and withdrew from Afghanistan. Abouhalima returned to the United States a battle-hardened believer in the Islamic revolution, ready to continue the jihad wherever it needed to be fought.

Back in the United States, Abouhalima became friendly with other veterans of the Afghanistan war. They would gather in the forests of Connecticut, north of New York, where they wore traditional Muslim robes and practiced firing AK-47 automatic rifles. Abouhalima also started praying at a mosque, a Muslim place of worship, in nearby Jersey City, New Jersey. The leader of the Jersey City mosque was Sheik Omar Abdel Rahman. Abouhalima became close to Rahman, serving as the cleric's driver and bodyguard.

Rahman was a large man who often needed assistance from others to walk. He was also blind. Like Abouhalima, he was born in Egypt. There he attended Al-Azar University, the Islamic world's most prestigious institution of higher learning. At some point, he turned to radical fundamentalism. Anwar Sadat had thrown him in prison several times before the Egyptian leader was assassinated in 1981. Clearly, Rahman had advocated violence.

"Hit hard and kill the enemies of God in every spot to rid the state of the descendants of the apes and pigs fed at the tables of Zionism, Communism and Imperialism," Rahman preached at one point.

✠   ✠   ✠

New York City is home to some of the tallest buildings in the world. The Empire State Building rises 1,250 feet from the street. Completed in 1931, it dominated the skyline of Manhattan for years, the tallest among the tall. But in 1976 the New York and New Jersey Port Authority, which oversees shipping and trade in New York City's busy riverfront harbors—completed an even taller office building: the World Trade Center.

The World Trade Center is actually seven buildings, the largest of which are the two main towers, each 110 floors. The towers stand 1,360 feet tall. During a typical day, some 50,000 people work in the Twin Towers and another 80,000 visit the complex, making the World Trade Center itself a city within a city. The entire complex covers 16 acres of Manhattan real estate.

To erect the World Trade Center, construction crews used 200,000 tons of steel and 425,000 cubic yards of cement—enough to pave a 200-mile sidewalk. It took 17 years to build the monumental complex.

Terrorists hoped only minutes would be needed to destroy it. Just after noon on February 26, 1993, a powerful bomb exploded in the World Trade Center's basement parking garage, killing six people and injuring 1,000. Prosecutors would later reveal that the terrorists hoped to topple one of the Twin Towers into the other, sending both structures falling like titanic dominoes into the Lower End of Manhattan and killing as many as 250,000 people.

The towers did not fall, but in the building above the parking garage, chaos reigned. Lights flickered, then went dark. Elevators stuck between floors. Smoke rose from the basement to infiltrate the building's ventilation system. In the parking garage, the bomb opened up a 200-foot crater in the concrete. Damage to the building was estimated at $650 million.

At first, authorities weren't sure the explosion had been caused by a bomb. Could there have been a gas leak? New York's governor, Mario Cuomo, didn't need convincing. "It looks like a bomb, it smells like a bomb—it's probably a bomb," Cuomo told reporters shortly after the blast. Cuomo suspected terrorists.

"No foreign people or force has ever done this to us," Cuomo said. "Until now, we were invulnerable."

Investigators soon confirmed Cuomo's suspicions. Sifting through the rubble in the parking garage, they came across a twisted piece of metal they identified as the chassis of a cargo van. Bomb experts inspected the chassis and concluded that it was at the center of the explosion. They estimated that the van held a 1,200-pound bomb made of the powerful explosive urea-nitrate.

Incredibly, on the chassis investigators were able to find the van's unique serial number, called a vehicle identification number. Once investigators had the vehicle identification number, it was a simple matter for them to trace the van to a truck rental agency in Jersey City, New Jersey. The van had been rented three days before the World Trade Center bombing by a man named Mohammed Salameh. Authorities apprehended Salameh when, claiming the van had been stolen, he returned to the truck rental agency to have his $200 deposit refunded.

In his pocket authorities found a copy of the rental contract he had filled out to obtain the van. And on that rental contract was residue from bomb-making chemicals.

Once Salameh had been arrested, things began falling into place. Investigators started looking into the activities of other radical fundamentalists, and the two names they kept hearing were Mahmud Abouhalima and Sheik Omar Abdel Rahman.

Abouhalima had boarded a plane for Egypt only hours after the bombing, but Egyptian police picked him up. Especially in cases involving terrorism, the Egyptian authorities have a reputation for not being particularly concerned about the niceties of suspects' rights. Abouhalima was apparently subjected to hours of torture. His 15-year-old brother, Sayed, was also picked up and tortured by the police, who warned Abouhalima that other family members would suffer the same treatment until he confessed. Finally, Abouhalima revealed his role in planning and enlisting others to carry out the World Trade Center bombing. The spiritual leader for the whole mission, he said, was Sheik Rahman.

After his confession, Abouhalima was returned to the United States, where 22 suspects, including Rahman, were arrested in connection with the World Trade Center bombing. As the investigation continued, police learned that the World Trade Center bombing wasn't the only act of terrorism the conspirators planned. They also had plans to bomb the Holland and Lincoln tunnels, the United Nations Building, and the FBI's headquarters in Lower Manhattan. Plus they intended to assassinate Egyptian president Hosni Mubarak and Senator Alfonse D'Amato, a strong supporter of Israel in the U.S. Congress.

Abouhalima, Rahman, and eight other conspirators were convicted in the World Trade Center bombing. They each received jail sentences of 240 years.

One terrorist who got away was Ramzi Ahmed Yousef, who had allegedly assembled the bomb. Like Abouhalima, Yousef boarded a plane headed overseas the day of the bombing. For more than a year his whereabouts remained unknown. He finally resurfaced on December 9, 1994, when he purchased a ticket for a Philippine Air Lines flight between Manila and Cebu. When he got off the plane in Cebu, Yousef left behind a bomb under his seat. The bomb exploded while the plane was en route to its final destination, Tokyo, killing a Japanese passenger and forcing the pilots to make an emergency landing.

Yousef was nearly arrested in Manila a month later when police raided room 603 of the Josefa Apartments, which overlooked the route Pope John Paul II intended to take for his planned visit to the Philippines. Inside the apartment, police found bomb-making equipment and chemicals, a map of the pope's route, priest's clothing, and airline schedules for trans-Pacific flights. Yousef was not home at the time of the raid—he had apparently been tipped off that the police were coming.

In February 1995, with a $2 million reward posted by the United States for his capture, Yousef turned up in Islamabad, Pakistan. He was apprehended in a hotel room, where police found bomb-making equipment, explosives, and flight schedules for American airplanes. Yousef was quickly flown to the United States to face justice. In 1997, he was convicted of setting the bomb that killed the Japanese passenger aboard the Philippine Air

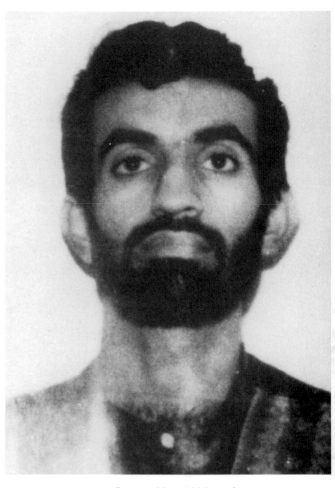

Ramzi Ahmed Yousef, who helped assemble the World Trade Center bomb, eluded authorities for two years. He was finally captured in Pakistan.

A Sudanese security officer surveys the remains of a pharmaceutical plant near Khartoum. After terrorist attacks on two U.S. embassies in East Africa, President Clinton ordered a cruise-missile strike on the plant, citing intelligence sources claiming that it had been manufacturing deadly nerve agents for terrorists.

Lines flight. A year later, he stood trial and was convicted for his role in the plot to blow up the World Trade Center. He received a sentence of 240 years.

At his sentencing in New York, Yousef was defiant. He offered no apologies for his actions and made little attempt to hide his hatred for the American prosecutors or the judge who would soon sentence him to the lengthy prison term.

"Yes, I am a terrorist, and I'm proud of it," Yousef said. "I support terrorism as long as it is used against the United States and Israel. You are more than terrorists. You are butchers, liars and hypocrites."

Although the World Trade Center conspirators were

now locked up, it would not be the end of fundamentalist-backed terrorism against the United States. During the investigation of the World Trade Center case, law enforcement agents turned up the name of a wealthy member of the Saudi Arabian ruling family who had embraced radical fundamentalism and led a group of militants to a mountain hideout in Afghanistan. His name was Osama bin Laden. Like Abouhalima, he had fought on the side of the mujahedin against the Soviets.

On August 7, 1998, terrorists used truck bombs to attack the U.S. embassies in two East African nations. In Dar es Salaam, Tanzania, 10 people were killed and dozens injured. The terrorist attack in Nairobi, Kenya, proved even more deadly. The bomber had attempted to crash a bomb-laden pickup truck into the embassy but had been turned back by gunfire from an embassy guard. The driver pulled into a nearby alley, where the vehicle suddenly exploded, collapsing a building that stood next to the American embassy. Twelve Americans and more than 250 Kenyans were killed, and some 5,000 people in the vicinity of the blast were injured. Osama bin Laden quickly announced that he had ordered the bombings.

The United States soon retaliated. President Bill Clinton ordered cruise-missile strikes against bin Laden's terrorist camp in Afghanistan as well as against a pharmaceutical plant in Khartoum, Sudan, that Central Intelligence Agency (CIA) sources believed was developing nerve gas for terrorists. The pharmaceutical plant was destroyed (although news reports later called into question the accuracy of the CIA's information that the plant had been making nerve agents). While bin Laden's terrorist base sustained heavy damage, the fundamentalist leader himself was not injured in the attack. Vowing to step up his terrorist attacks on the United States, he remained beyond the reach of American justice.

"Something Big Is Going to Happen"

6

*T*he *Turner Diaries* is a chilling account of a world gone mad. The book, published in 1978, takes the form of a diary kept by a participant in the cataclysmic events that unfold. The book starts with a bombing of FBI headquarters in Washington. Soon tensions escalate into a nuclear war between the United States and the Soviet Union. The war kills billions of people, wiping out virtually the entire populations of Europe, North America, South America, Asia, and Africa.

There are survivors, though. Out of this nuclear holocaust an "Aryan Republic" forms. It is a society based on the racist Nazi regime that tried to conquer Europe and ignited World War II in 1939. In history, Adolf Hitler and his Nazi followers were defeated. But in *The Turner Diaries*, the Aryan survivors of the nuclear war triumph, forcing millions of people onto work farms, where they are turned into slaves. Yet for Turner, the book's protagonist, it is all worth it.

"What a miracle it is to walk the streets which only a few weeks ago were filled with non-whites lounging on every street corner in every doorway and to see only white faces—clean, happy, enthusiastic white faces, determined and hopeful for the future," writes Turner.

The author of *The Turner Diaries*, William L. Pierce, is a white supremacist and organizer of the National Alliance, a West Virginia–based neo-Nazi group. Since its publication, *The Turner Diaries* has rarely been sold in mainstream bookstores. But the book has generated an underground cult following among right-wing militias, neo-Nazis, and other hate groups. It is mostly available through mail order from organizations that promote racist ideas.

Timothy McVeigh read *The Turner Diaries*. He regarded it as the most important book ever written. He read it while serving in the U.S. Army and would readily loan out his copy to friends. After he left the army, McVeigh sold copies of *The Turner Diaries* at gun shows, often taking a loss on the sales simply because he thought it was important for the book's message to circulate. On April 19, 1995, when a police officer in Perry, Oklahoma, pulled McVeigh over because the car he was driving had no license plate, a copy of *The Turner Diaries* was sitting on the backseat.

✠   ✠   ✠

By the end of the 20th century, terrorism had come full circle. A hundred years earlier, Emma Goldman and Alexander Berkman had urged their followers to use violence to establish a new social order based on the principles of communism: that workers were abused and exploited by wealthy people and the governments they

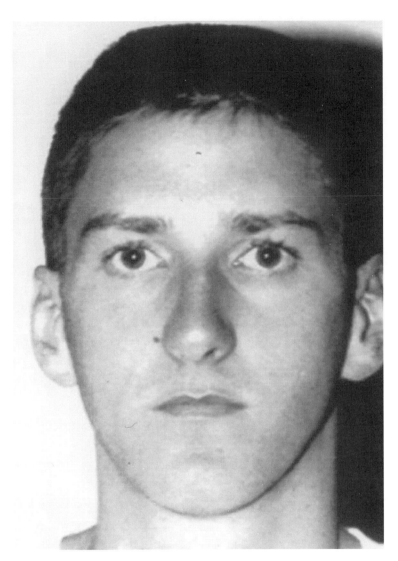

Timothy McVeigh, a young army veteran, was an avid reader of *The Turner Diaries*, a white-supremacist novel that opens with the destruction of FBI headquarters in Washington, D.C., by a homemade ammonium nitrate bomb.

controlled. "Lousy capitalists!" the would-be presidential assassin Guiseppe Zangara shouted to his executioners shortly before the death penalty was carried out.

In the 1980s and 1990s, the message may have been similar, but the messenger was quite different. Now it was a right-wing movement, not Communists, who claimed that big corporations and the U.S. government were conspiring to oppress them. At the paranoid fringes of this movement—known as the militia move-

The Branch Davidian compound in flames, April 19, 1993. More than 70 members of the religious cult perished in the inferno, which began when the FBI attempted to use tear gas to force the Davidians out. Enraged by what he viewed as the government's heavy-handed treatment of the Davidians, McVeigh chose the two-year anniversary of the Waco debacle to bomb the Murrah federal building.

ment—conspiracy theories abound: that the government sends black helicopters over small towns to spy on militia members, that road signs include tiny bar codes intended to give foreign armies directions once they invade America, that the ultimate goal of the federal government is to band together with other nations to form a single world government. The beliefs of more-mainstream militia members are less outlandish but share the same antigovernment theme. They feel that the federal government is too involved in citizens' every-day lives, imposing taxes and myriad laws and regulations that infringe on personal freedoms. But the central tenet of the militia movement—as the name would suggest—is that Americans have an absolute right to gun ownership under the Second Amendment to the U.S. Constitution, and that contrary to that constitutional guarantee the government is trying to disarm its citizens. Its purpose, militia members argue, is to eliminate resistance to future acts of government tyranny.

Guns and supposed government tyranny were at the center of two controversial incidents that galvanized the militia movement. In 1992, federal agents tried to arrest a white supremacist named Randy Weaver, who was wanted on gun charges, at his cabin in remote Ruby Ridge, Idaho. After a gunfight in which a U.S. marshal and Weaver's 14-year-old son Samuel died, Weaver barricaded his family inside the cabin. After a long siege, a federal agent shot into the cabin and killed Weaver's wife, Vicki. Vicki and Samuel Weaver soon became martyrs to people in the militia movement.

The following year, another law enforcement siege produced dozens of martyrs for the militia movement. On February 28, 1993, agents from the U.S. Bureau of Alcohol, Tobacco and Firearms (ATF) raided the 73-acre compound of a religious group known as the Branch Davidians in Waco, Texas. The ATF agents were attempting to serve a warrant on the Davidians' leader—a self-styled messiah who called himself David Koresh—for weapons violations. But a gunfight erupted, during which four ATF agents and several Davidians were killed before the ATF withdrew. Soon the FBI took charge of the Waco situation, surrounding the compound and attempting to negotiate the surrender of Koresh and his followers. Weeks passed with no progress. Finally, on April 19, 1993—50 days after the ill-fated ATF raid—the FBI used a tank to smash through the wall of the Davidians' main building and pump in tear gas. The tear gas failed to flush the Davidians out, however. Instead, fire swept through the compound, and more than 70 Davidians, including 17 children, perished. The FBI insisted that the Davidians themselves had set the fire in a mass suicide. Critics disputed the official story.

To Timothy McVeigh, Waco was just another example of how the government trampled the rights of innocent Americans. April 19 would become burned in his mind.

By all accounts, McVeigh had led a quiet, unremarkable life while growing up in Pendleton, New York, about 15 miles northeast of Niagara Falls. After high school, he joined the army in May 1988. He became friends with another man who had joined the army the same day: Terry Nichols, a native of rural Kansas. McVeigh and Nichols were assigned to the same unit at Fort Benning, Georgia, and later at Fort Riley, Kansas.

Although his friend Terry Nichols left the army in 1989, McVeigh continued to serve. He was sent to the Persian Gulf and saw action during Operation Desert Storm in 1991, winning a Bronze Star. But he was also a loner who never seemed to have a girlfriend, never talked about his family, and kept to the barracks, where he watched television and immersed himself in magazines about guns. He was apparently obsessed with guns, often keeping a 9-mm handgun in the barracks with him, which was against army rules. His private collection also included a machine gun from the Czech Republic as well as assorted pistols, shotguns, and rifles, which he kept stashed in the trunk of his car. In 1991, he applied to the army's elite Special Forces unit—the fabled Green Berets—and was turned down. That experience soured McVeigh on an army career, and he left the service on December 31, 1991. Soon after, he sent a letter to a friend. On the paper, McVeigh had drawn a picture of a skull and crossbones. The letter read: "So many victims, so little time."

Returning home to Pendleton, McVeigh worked on and off as a security guard. He was discontented with

American society and government and became a supporter of the right-wing militias. While he seemed to do
little but mark time, he did write letters to a local newspaper, the *Union-Sun and Journal* of Lockport, New
York. In one letter he claimed, "The American dream of
the middle class has all but disappeared, substituted with
people struggling just to buy groceries. Do we have to
shed blood to reform the current system? I hope it
doesn't come to that. But it might." Another letter asked,
"Is civil war imminent?"

Sometime in 1992, McVeigh left Pendleton and
moved in with Terry Nichols and his brother Jim at Jim
Nichols's farm in Michigan. A fourth man, Michael
Fortier, also lived at the Nichols farm during this period.
Next, McVeigh showed up in Kingman, Arizona, where
he moved into a mobile home.

By 1993, McVeigh was making his living selling guns,
ammunition, and other arms at gun shows, which are
typically held in venues such as hotel ballrooms and exhi-
bition centers, and are for the most part unregulated by
state or federal authorities. McVeigh was selling arms
through the mail as well.

He was also watching movies. One film he took in
was *Brazil*, a comedy about a future society dominated by
faceless bureaucrats. *Brazil* features a character named
Tuttle, played by Robert De Niro, who becomes a terrorist and blows up a government building. McVeigh started
going by the name Tuttle, even using it in an ad he ran in
a right-wing magazine offering a military grenade
launcher for sale.

Soon after the incident in Waco, McVeigh is believed
to have traveled to Elohim City, a hardscrabble compound of cabins built into the rugged terrain of eastern
Oklahoma near the Arkansas border. Elohim City was
founded by an elderly Canadian minister named Robert

McVeigh's ammonium nitrate bomb, estimated at 5,000 pounds and concealed in a rented Ryder truck, produced enough force to collapse an entire side of the Murrah building.

Millar, who believes New Year's Day occurs on March 20, Christmas is in October, and whites of northern European descent are God's chosen people. Ironically, *Elohim* is a Hebrew word for God. Millar has claimed he has no knowledge that McVeigh ever lived in Elohim City, but witnesses have said somebody fitting McVeigh's description and traveling under the name Tuttle did stay in the encampment.

In April 1995, McVeigh checked into room 25 of the Dreamland Motel in Junction City, Kansas. He rented a truck and parked it on the motel parking lot. On Sunday, April 16, McVeigh called Terry Nichols at his home in Herington, Kansas, asking his friend to pick him up in Oklahoma City and drive him the 270 miles to Junction City.

"Something big is going to happen," McVeigh told Nichols.

"Are you going to rob a bank?" Nichols asked.

McVeigh answered by simply repeating, "Something big is going to happen."

Two days later, McVeigh again called Nichols. The two drove to a storage shed McVeigh had leased. Inside were bags of ammonium nitrate, a chemical commonly used as a fertilizer. Also inside were an antitank rocket, 33 guns, bomb detonators, 55-gallon plastic drums, books about the Waco incident, and antigovernment pamphlets.

"If I don't come back in a while, you clean out the storage shed," McVeigh told Nichols.

On April 19, 1995—the second anniversary of the FBI raid on the Branch Davidian compound in Waco— McVeigh drove his rented truck to Oklahoma City, leaving it in the parking lot of the Alfred P. Murrah Federal Building. Inside the back of the truck was a homemade bomb weighing an estimated 5,000 pounds.

Just after 9 A.M., when hundreds of federal employees were at their desks in the Murrah building, the bomb detonated. A red-orange fireball lit up the sky, and the entire north side of the Murrah building disintegrated. Glass from windows shot out in every direction, slashing into innocent victims like knives. The shock waves ripped parking meters from the ground. Roofs on nearby buildings collapsed. Metal doors folded as though they were slips of paper.

Across the country in Washington, President Bill Clinton was meeting with Tansu Ciller, the prime minister of Turkey. Ironically, the issue being discussed by the two leaders was Turkey's attack on Kurdish rebels in northern Iraq, which Ciller insisted was done to combat terrorism in her country. A White House aide rushed into the room, leaned over, and told President Clinton that the CNN television network had just reported that an explosion had leveled a federal building in Oklahoma City. Clinton told the aide to find out what he could.

Minutes later, another aide slipped the president a note. It read: "Half of federal building in Oklahoma City blown up—expect heavy casualties."

Indeed, the number of casualties would be high: 168 people died in the blast, making it the largest death toll from a single act of terrorism committed on American soil. Many of the victims were young children and infants who were staying in the Murrah building's second-floor day care center.

An hour and a half after the blast, as rescue workers treated the injured and began the arduous search for survivors underneath the tons of rubble that had been the Murrah building, a police officer pulled McVeigh over in Perry, Oklahoma. When he approached the car, the policeman noticed that the driver was wearing a shoulder harness holding a semiautomatic pistol. The gun turned out to be loaded with deadly hollow-point bullets. McVeigh was quickly arrested and charged with carrying a concealed weapon. Within days, he would become the prime suspect in the Oklahoma City bombing.

Meanwhile, the search for buried survivors continued. Units from the U.S. Air Force, National Guard, and FBI soon arrived. Sixty firefighters from Arizona who specialized in finding victims in collapsed buildings were called in. Cranes and backhoes were driven onto the site to remove the rubble. Right behind them came specialists to operate listening devices to detect signs of life in the debris. Specially trained dogs were led into the wreckage to help sniff out victims. Every few minutes the order would go out to shut down the equipment so that the lis-

An Oklahoma City firefighter searches for victims amid the rubble. The death toll from the blast would ultimately reach 168.

tening devices could operate. Occasionally, the equipment did find a victim, still alive and trapped under tons of concrete and steel. The rescue teams worked throughout the day, and when night fell they set up huge floodlights so they could work at night. The rescue workers used heavy equipment, shovels, pickaxes, and their bare hands. Sometimes they could move no more than an inch or two of rubble at a time.

While the terrible and heart-wrenching job of removing the victims from the rubble proceeded, special teams of explosives experts started examining the scene. They began with the 30-foot crater in front of the building, which was obviously where the blast had originated. Here they found two important clues: traces of ammonium nitrate and, in an eerie coincidence that made the investigators recall the World Trade Center bombing, a mangled and twisted truck chassis.

The traces of ammonium nitrate—a common fertilizer that can be bought in most gardening stores for about 11 cents a pound—told them that the blast was caused by a homemade bomb. When mixed with fuel oil, ammonium nitrate becomes a powerful explosive that can be detonated with a blasting cap. Constructing a so-called fertilizer bomb takes some skill and knowledge of explosives, but instructions can be obtained on the Internet or found in such books on terrorism as *The Anarchist Cookbook*.

Just as in the World Trade Center case, investigators found the vehicle identification number from the mangled chassis of the rental truck containing the bomb. And once they had the vehicle identification number, it didn't take them long to trace the truck to Timothy McVeigh, who was at the moment being held in a tiny jail in Perry after his traffic stop. With cooperation from Michael Fortier, who had lived with McVeigh and Terry Nichols on Jim Nichols's farm, investigators built cases against the former army buddies. After a three-month federal trial, McVeigh was convicted of eight counts of murder (eight of the victims had been federal agents), conspiracy to use a weapon of mass destruction, using a weapon of mass destruction, and destruction of a federal building. He was sentenced to death. Terry Nichols, who prosecutors said had helped McVeigh assemble the bomb and who left McVeigh's getaway car in Oklahoma City, was convicted of one count of conspiracy and eight counts of involuntary manslaughter. He was sentenced to life in prison. Michael Fortier pleaded guilty to helping McVeigh raise cash to purchase the bomb materials. In return for his testimony against McVeigh and Nichols, he received a relatively lenient sentence of 12 years in prison.

Timothy McVeigh's lawyers have filed appeals as he awaits execution by lethal injection. He has admitted nothing. He regards himself as a political prisoner and continues to insist that the U.S. government is at the bottom of a plot to wipe out the rights of innocent Americans.

Shortly before he went on trial, the *Dallas Morning News* reported that one of McVeigh's attorneys asked him why he hadn't bombed the Murrah building at night, when the building would have been mostly vacant and much fewer people would have died.

"That would not have gotten the point across to the government," McVeigh reportedly told his lawyer. "We needed a body count to make our point."

The War on Terrorism

A traveler passes through an experimental explosives-detection portal at the Albuquerque International Airport in New Mexico. High technology can be a powerful weapon, but it alone will never win the war against terrorism.

The United States is the world's foremost power. Its economic, cultural, and military influence is felt all over the globe. In some quarters this prominence has bred resentment and made America a target for terrorists.

The United States is also an open society that protects the right of free speech, places no restrictions on freedom of movement, limits the powers of law enforcement, and guarantees certain rights to all criminal suspects. To a certain extent, all this makes the job of combating terrorism more difficult.

Free speech and the free flow of information mean that people who might be inclined to commit acts of terrorism, if they are even moderately resourceful, will be able to find out how. For example, anyone with a computer and a modem can find instructions for creating a fertilizer bomb on the Internet (and the major ingredients are readily and legally available). Of course, one need not even have a computer, as various how-to anarchist books also contain instructions for a fertilizer bomb. And it was this type of simple, low-tech explosive that Timothy McVeigh used to author the deadliest terrorist attack ever on American soil.

Within the borders of their country, Americans are free to go virtually anywhere, with no travel documents. Similarly, once foreigners have entered the United States, they can move about pretty much as they please; unless for some reason they come to the attention of law enforcement authorities, no one keeps tabs on their whereabouts or activities. There is no question that this freedom of movement creates opportunities for terrorists.

In America the potential for terrorism is also increased by limits on the powers of law enforcement officials. The U.S. Constitution prohibits police from subjecting Americans to random stops or searches. Police may not tap a person's phone or search his or her house without a court-issued warrant, and to obtain that warrant they must show probable cause for believing that the person has committed a crime. Once in custody, suspects are guaranteed certain rights, including the right to legal counsel and the right against self-incrimination, and police may not obtain confessions through coercive means. Not every nation grants such rights, and as a result fighting terrorism in those nations may be somewhat less complicated. In Egypt, for example, Mahmud Abouhalima confessed his role in the World Trade Center bombing and implicated his coconspirators after authorities tortured him and his brother. In the United States that treatment would never be permitted.

Of course, law enforcement officers don't always comply with the Constitution. For example, in 1919 the

Red Raiders trampled the rights of suspected anarchists. But such constitutional violations in the name of fighting terrorism have very much been the exception, and in the United States illegal police conduct is always subject to scrutiny by the courts.

In recent years combating terrorism has seemed especially important, particularly in the wake of such disasters as the Oklahoma City bombing and the 1988 bombing of Pan Am Flight 103 over Lockerbie, Scotland—which claimed the lives of 259 passengers and crew, most of them Americans, along with 11 people on the ground. In addition, experts have cautioned that in

A Scottish police officer walks past the fuselage of the Boeing 747 jumbo jet that exploded in midair and crashed near the town of Lockerbie on December 21, 1988. It took a seven-year international trade embargo to convince Libyan dictator Muammar Qaddafi to turn over two suspects in the Pan Am Flight 103 bombing.

the near future terrorists may turn away from the low-tech weapons used by Timothy McVeigh and the World Trade Center conspirators in favor of infinitely more lethal chemical, biological, or even nuclear weapons. But a terrorist could wreak havoc without any weapons, and without even physically being in the United States, by hacking into one of the many computer networks that regulate American financial, transportation, or communications systems. So the stakes in heading off potential terrorist threats are very high.

Still, comparatively little actual terrorism has taken place in the United States, and the price of completely wiping out the threat of terrorism would be higher than most Americans are willing to pay. It would likely require the forfeiture of some individual liberties and constitutional protections, along with an expansion of police surveillance powers. The inevitable result would be a more intrusive law enforcement presence in citizens' everyday lives. It has been observed, correctly, that only a police state can promise freedom from terrorism.

So a balance must be struck between preserving the benefits of an open society and protecting against terrorist attacks, achieving the maximum security possible while still guaranteeing cherished individual rights. In recent years, government agencies and commercial organizations have taken many steps to combat terrorism. Some of them are readily apparent. For example, before Lolita Lebron and her fellow terrorists carried out their attack on the U.S. House of Representatives in 1954, they strolled into the Capitol carrying concealed guns. A guard at the Visitors Gallery asked them only whether they were carrying cameras. Today visitors must pass through metal detectors before entering the Capitol and must obtain passes to enter the House and Senate galleries; some corridors in the Capitol are completely off-limits to visitors. In the parking lots outside the House and Senate office buildings nearby, huge concrete barricades have been installed, which are intended to prevent a suicide bomber from ramming a car into the buildings. Across town, at the White House, Pennsylvania Avenue is closed to vehicular traffic, to prevent a suicide bomber from driving a vehicle laden with explosives through the front gates of the Executive Mansion. At other government installations throughout the country, police have closed off streets surrounding the buildings.

Antiterrorist measures have been taken at commercial sites as well. For example, more than 350 private security officers now patrol the World Trade Center in New York, and employees there must wear photo identification badges. Except for the rooftop observation platforms and the restaurants, the Twin Towers are no longer open to the public. Dozens of security cameras have been installed, and in the garage—the scene of the blast in 1993—access is limited to police officers and World Trade Center workers with passes.

Travelers have also noticed changes since the Lockerbie bombing and other acts of terrorism directed at airlines. Passengers on international flights have to arrive at airports earlier to go through extensive screening. Once a passenger checks in, he or she may not leave a terminal and return again, and no unattended luggage may be loaded onto a plane.

And yet, at public places such as airports, offices, and government buildings, no precautions will stop every potential attacker. Russell Weston Jr. proved this on July 24, 1998. Armed with a handgun, Weston ran past a metal detector into the U.S. Capitol, murdering two policemen and wounding a tourist before being cut down by a policeman's bullet. Though Weston was mentally ill, not a terrorist, his actions demonstrate the

The effort to prevent terrorism takes many forms. This page: A concrete barrier is lowered into place near the base of the Washington Monument. Opposite page: Using a handheld metal detector at the United Nations.

limits of technology and vigilance in eliminating the threat of terrorism.

While antiterrorism measures like physical barriers around government buildings and stricter procedures for air travel are straightforward and highly visible, much of the war against terrorism is fought out of public view. In laboratories scientists work to create the tools and

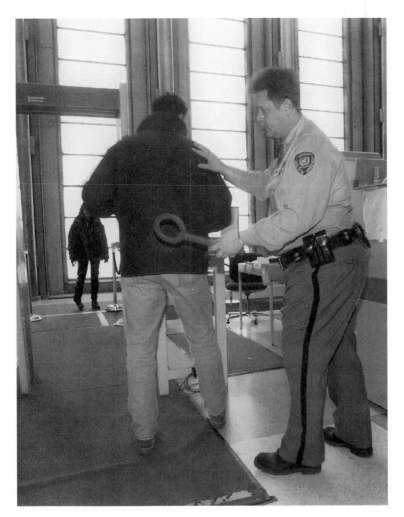

weapons the authorities need to confront terrorists.
Among the devices and systems under development are
portable scanning systems that can identify the chemical
composition of items in closed containers, which could
prove especially useful for checking luggage at airports;
bullets composed of superheated aluminum and water
that might be chemically adjusted to stun, disable, or
kill—which if perfected could lessen the risk to hostages
during terrorist incidents; a highly adhesive foam that
could be sprayed on terrorists to immobilize them; an all-
terrain robotic vehicle that could be operated via video

Firefighters in Greenville, South Carolina, practice how to deal with a terrorist attack using biological weapons. Preparation and vigilance on the part of law enforcement are important, but in an open society like the United States there is no guarantee that terrorists won't be able to launch a deadly attack.

hookup from up to 2,000 miles away, which could be sent into an area that has been contaminated with deadly biological or chemical agents; nano-bombs—microscopic droplets of oil that researchers say will bond to deadly but easy-to-produce anthrax germs, causing them literally to explode and become harmless; and advanced software to warn when a hacker has entered a computer system.

In addition to the scientific effort, the war against terrorism is fought in the legislative and diplomatic arenas. In 1984 and 1986, Congress passed legislation making it a crime under U.S. law to harm American citizens for political purposes anywhere in the world. The laws authorized the FBI to investigate terrorism against U.S. citizens in other countries and to make arrests. With the cooperation of other countries, the terrorists could then be extradited, or returned to the United States to stand trial. The laws also authorized the State Department to post rewards of up to $2 million for information leading to the capture of terrorists. The reward program paid dividends in 1995 when a tip helped police track down World Trade Center terrorist Ramzi Ahmed Yousef in Pakistan.

Congress took further aim at terrorism in 1996, when it passed the Antiterrorism and Effective Death Penalty Act. One of the major goals of the act was to choke off financial support for terrorists, even if that support was indirect. Thus the act prohibited financial transactions between American citizens and countries that support international terrorism, forbade U.S. banks from acting as depositories for money controlled by terrorist groups, and made it a crime for American citizens to give financial or material support to any foreign organization the U.S. secretary of state designates as terrorist, even if the support is for humanitarian purposes. People found in violation of the act are subject to lengthy prison terms.

Terrorism is a thoroughly international problem: for example, terrorists headquartered in one country may launch an attack against citizens of another country on the territory of a third country. For this reason, no nation can hope to combat terrorism alone. The United States has worked with a number of countries to forge treaties and agreements to bring terrorists to justice, and in several high-profile cases the international cooperation has paid off. In 1985, for example, PLO terrorists who had hijacked an Italian cruise ship, the *Achille Lauro*, and murdered an American tourist were apprehended as the result of cooperation between Israeli, American, and Italian authorities. After trading their hostages for a jetliner, the terrorists were en route to Tunisia when U.S. military planes tipped off by Israeli intelligence forced them to land in Italy. That same year, West Germany tried and convicted Mohammed Hammadei, an Islamic terrorist who had participated in the skyjacking of a TWA plane during which a U.S. Navy diver was murdered. More recently, in 1999, United Nations–sponsored economic sanctions against Libya finally forced that country's leader, Muammar Qaddafi, to turn over two Libyan suspects in the 1988 Pan Am Flight 103 bombing. The suspects were to be tried in the Netherlands under Scottish law.

International cooperation has its limits, however. Sometimes terrorists find safe haven in countries that have no extradition treaties or that actively support terrorism. What to do when terrorists are beyond the reach of organized justice becomes a difficult question for government policymakers.

Israel has always taken a firm and unequivocal stance. When a terrorist attack occurs, it retaliates against the group it believes is responsible. And, when individuals responsible can be identified but can't be brought to justice in the courts, Israel hunts them down and tries to kill them. In the months and years after Black September's terrorist attack during the 1972 Summer Olympics, for example, agents from Israel's Mossad tracked down and murdered Black September officials throughout Europe and the Middle East.

Because of political and ethical considerations, it is not U.S. policy—nor, so far as is known, practice—to murder individual terrorists. But two presidents, Ronald Reagan and Bill Clinton, have ordered military strikes in retaliation for terrorist acts. In April 1986, after intelligence sources pointed to Libyan involvement in the bombing of a West Berlin discotheque frequented by American servicemen, Reagan ordered air strikes against Libyan military targets and the compound of Muammar

Qaddafi. And in August 1998, following the truck-bomb attacks on the U.S. embassies in Dar es Salaam and Nairobi, Clinton authorized cruise-missile attacks on the Sudanese pharmaceutical plant and Osama bin Laden's base in Afghanistan.

The effectiveness of this kind of retaliation in deterring future terrorism is unclear. What is certain is that the problem of terrorism will not soon disappear.

EPILOGUE

On September 11, 2001 the United States suffered the worst terrorist attacks in its history. At 8:45 A.M. a hijacked airliner, American Airlines Flight 11, crashed into the north tower of the World Trade Center. Minutes later at 9:03 A.M. a second hijacked airliner, United Airlines Flight 175, crashed into the south tower. The nation watched in horror as both towers collapsed within the hour. At 9:43 A.M., American Airlines Flight 77 crashed into the Pentagon. Thousands of lives were lost in both attacks.

Osama bin Laden and his terrorist organization al Qaeda are the prime suspects in the September 11th attacks. Since the attacks, the United States government has launched "Operation Enduring Freedom," which is a military campaign designed to rid the world of terrorism.

Chronology

1901	Anarchist Leon Czolgosz assassinates President William McKinley at the Pan American Exposition in Buffalo, New York
1919	A series of anarchist bombings leads Attorney General A. Mitchell Palmer to initiate the "Red Raids"
1920	Thirty-eight people killed when an anarchist's bomb explodes on Wall Street in New York
1933	Chicago mayor Anton Cermak fatally wounded during anarchist Guiseppe Zangara's unsuccessful attempt to assassinate Franklin D. Roosevelt
1950	Puerto Rican terrorists try to assassinate President Harry S. Truman
1954	Three Puerto Rican terrorists spray the U.S. House of Representatives with bullets, wounding five congressmen
1972	Eleven Israeli athletes, five Black September terrorists, and a German police officer die in terrorist incident during the Summer Olympics
1973	Marcus Foster, superintendent of schools in Oakland, California, shot to death by a group of terrorists who call themselves the Symbionese Liberation Army (SLA)
1974	Newspaper heiress Patricia Campbell Hearst is kidnapped by the SLA on February 4; on April 15, Hearst participates in the SLA robbery of the Hibernia National Bank in San Francisco; on May 17, five SLA members, including founder Donald DeFreeze, die in a shoot-out with Los Angeles police
1975	On January 24, four people die and 60 are injured when a bomb set by the FALN, a Puerto Rican terrorist group, explodes in New York City's historic Fraunces Tavern; on September 18, Patty Hearst captured in San Francisco with SLA members Wendy Yoshimura and Bill and Emily Harris
1976	Seven terrorists skyjack an Air France jet en route to Israel and force the plane to land in Entebbe, Uganda; Israel dispatches a commando team, which frees the hostages and kills the terrorists

1981	Egyptian president Anwar Sadat assassinated by four soldiers; fundamentalist cleric Sheik Omar Abdel Rahman later arrested and charged with issuing a fatwa ordering Sadat's death, but he is eventually acquitted, leaves Egypt, and settles in Jersey City, New Jersey
1992	White supremacist Randy Weaver surrenders after a long siege by federal agents on his cabin in Ruby Ridge, Idaho
1993	On February 26, fundamentalist Muslim extremists explode a truck bomb in the basement garage of the World Trade Center in New York; FBI siege of the Branch Davidian compound in Waco, Texas, ends on April 19 with the deaths of 71 cult members
1995	On April 19, exactly two years after the Waco disaster, a truck bomb explodes in front of the Alfred P. Murrah Federal Building in Oklahoma City, killing 168 people
1996	Congress passes the Antiterrorism and Effective Death Penalty Act, giving federal law enforcement agencies sweeping new powers to investigate and prosecute people who assist terrorists
1998	U.S. embassies in Nairobi, Kenya, and Dar es Salaam, Tanzania, are attacked by suicide bombers; President Clinton orders cruise-missile strikes in retaliation
2000	Suicide bombing of the *U.S.S. Cole* kills 17 U.S. sailors
2001	
June	Convicted Oklahoma City bomber Timothy McVeigh is put to death by lethal injection
September	The United States suffers its worst terrorist attack in history; Three hijacked planes crash into the Word Trade Center and the Pentagon on September 11th, killing thousands; Osama bin Laden and his terrorist organization al Qaeda are the prime suspects; Operation Enduring Freedom is launched to combat terrorism worldwide
October	The four men convicted of the carrying out the truck bomb attacks on the U.S. Embassies in Tanzania and Kenya are sentenced to life in prison

Further Reading

Carr, Raymond. *Puerto Rico: A Colonial Experiment.* New York: Vintage, 1984.

Clarke, James W. *American Assassins: The Darker Side of Politics.* Princeton, N.J.: Princeton University Press, 1984.

Gaines, Ann G. *Terrorism.* Philadelphia: Chelsea House Publishers, 1999.

Goines, David. *The Free Speech Movement.* Berkeley, Calif.: Ten Speed Press, 1993.

Goldman, Emma. *Living My Life.* New York: Dover Publications, Inc., 1970.

Graff, James L. "The White City on a Hill." *Time*, February 24, 1997.

Hearst, Patricia Campbell. *Every Secret Thing.* Garden City, N.Y.: Doubleday & Co., Inc., 1982.

Heymann, Philip B. *Terrorism and America.* Cambridge, Mass.: The MIT Press, 1998.

McKay, Jim. *The Real McKay.* New York: Dutton, 1998.

Methven, Eugene H. "Hide and Seek." *National Review*, December 8, 1997.

Nash, Jay Robert. *Terrorism in the 20th Century.* New York: M. Evans and Co., Inc., 1998.

Phillips, Andrew. "The City of God Mystery." *MacLean's*, April 7, 1997.

Stickney, Brandon M. *All-American Monster: The Unauthorized Biography of Timothy McVeigh.* New York: Prometheus Books, 1996.

Weed, Steven. *My Search for Patty Hearst.* New York: Crown, 1976.

Websites

Anti-Defamation League.
"Counterterrorism at Home."
http://www.adl.org/frames/front_terrorism_up.html

Anti-Defamation League.
"Questions and Answers on the Turner Diaries."
http://www.adl.org/PresRele/Militi_71/2737_71.html

Latino Link.
http://www.latinolink.com

"Lolita Lebron at the U.N."
http://www.workers.org/ww/lebron.html

National Security Institute.
"Backgrounder: Terrorism."
http://nsi.org/library/terrorism/facterr.html

"Paranoia as Patriotism: Far-Right Influences on the Militia Movement."
*http://www1.us.nizkor.org/hweb/orgs/american/adl/
paranoia-as-patriotism/elohim-city.html*

Index

Index

Picture Credits

HAL MARCOVITZ is an award-winning journalist for the *Allentown Morning Call* in Pennsylvania. In 1993 and 1996, his columns were awarded Keystone Press Awards by the Pennsylvania Newspaper Publishers Association. He is the author of the satirical novel *Painting the White House*. His previous books for Chelsea House include biographies of the explorers Marco Polo and Francisco Vásquez de Coronado and actor Robin Williams. He makes his home in Chalfont, Pa., with his wife, Gail, and daughters Michelle and Ashley.

JILL McCAFFREY has served for four years as national chairman of the Armed Forces Emergency Services of the American Red Cross. Ms. McCaffrey also serves on the board of directors for Knollwood—the Army Distaff Hall. The former Jill Ann Faulkner, a Massachusetts native, is the wife of Barry R. McCaffrey, a member of President Bill Clinton's cabinet and director of the White House Office of National Drug Control Policy. The McCaffreys are the parents of three grown children: Sean, a major in the U.S. Army; Tara, an intensive care nurse and captain in the National Guard; and Amy, a seventh grade teacher. The McCaffreys also have two grandchildren, Michael and Jack.